The author of *Worlds Within Worlds* began her writing career in 1995. Her two-volume biography of the French 19th-century opera singer Pauline Viardot Garcia was published in 2004 and 2012, and includes a CD of songs by Viardot sung by the author. She also broadcasts on BBC Radio Jersey and writes articles on a variety of subjects. The material for this book dates from 1973 but it was first published in 2014 as *Life Is Everlasting* on Amazon Kindle. It has now been revised and re-titled as *Worlds Within Worlds*, published by Austin Macauley.

To those who gave me their support: Maria, Christine, Giles, Jillian, Eleanor, Angela, Alex, Peter, Sarah, Robin, Janice, Joan and E My Thursday group.

Barbara Kendall-Davies

WORLDS WITHIN WORLDS

AUSTIN MACAULEY PUBLISHERS™

LONDON ∗ CAMBRIDGE ∗ NEW YORK ∗ SHARJAH

A CIP catalogue record for this title is available from the British Library.

ISBN 9781528922029 (Paperback)
ISBN 9781528923200 (ePub e-book)

www.austinmacauley.com

First Published (2021)
Austin Macauley Publishers Ltd
25 Canada Square
Canary Wharf
London
E14 5LQ

Thanks to all my friends who continued to believe in my sanity!!!

Table of Contents

Introduction

This book is based on messages from people now living in another dimension. We refer to them as 'dead', yet in their own environment they are very much alive.

When people die, either because their loved ones are overcome with grief or they doubt an afterlife, the discarnate feel abandoned, especially when their names are no longer mentioned. However, when someone moves to another country efforts are made to stay in touch. All humans have the propensity to develop telepathy but it takes a focussed mind and commitment to forge the link necessary to reach into another dimension.

A well-known saying is 'the bourne from which no traveller returns' but it is a misconception. The physical brain decays with the body but the mind is eternal and far-reaching. Through telepathy, symbols or sign contacts with the physical world are sought. Even perfume can play its part and many people have experienced the sudden smell of a loved one's favourite flowers, of a cigarette or cigar, or even the smell of wet fish but dismiss them as imagination or coincidence.

It is possible that other dimensions occupy the same space as we do but like radio programmes have different frequencies, we could be interweaving with each other all the time without knowing it. The immediate post mortem state appears to be close to the Earth vibration but the discarnate later move on to a faster frequency so it is not so easy to receive their messages. Although initiates have always known such things, orthodox science has still to catch up. Even a century ago, something as common to us as the Internet would have been considered impossible.

Pictures are projected into the mind of someone still on Earth by a kind of holographic method but telepathy is the most usual form of contact. Just as some people are born with a facility for mathematics, writing, art or music, others have a more developed sixth sense. Psychic energies are fleeting which is why phenomena are difficult to sustain, particularly in laboratory conditions. The best method of developing the ability to move between dimensions is through the practice of meditation.

The source of inspiration is another mystery, though it is of great importance to creative artists, musicians, actors, writers, poets, historians, archaeologists, inventors and scientists because they rely on it whether they are aware or not. Just because people have dropped their earthly overcoat, they do not ditch their passions and skills, and many want to help kindred spirits who are still on Earth.

In cases of unfinished business, discarnate individuals will strive to make contact, especially in the case of missing wills or other lost documents, and evidence is well documented. My sister had a dream in which a friend who had been dead for several years showed her where a lost policy was situated, though it was in a place that had been quite overlooked.

Through the ages, natural psychics have reported communications with other realms of being, though in earlier times it was dangerous to admit psychic ability.

It is true that we have to leave all material things behind when we 'change channels' but we take the most important thing with us, our consciousness, which moves into another body, relevant to the new dimension. This subtle body is with us in life but is on a much faster frequency than the physical body so cannot be perceived with normal sight.

In describing a metaphysical realm, we are limited by our earthly vocabulary, yet the communicators in this book have managed to convey some of their other world experiences. In simple language, they help us to appreciate what to expect when we move on. However, every person is an individual, so the conditions vary from person to person and what is experienced is conditioned by the state of the mind of the individual. Those who have developed their creativity and imagination will soon adjust to the new conditions but those who have lived purely within the material world will need a good deal of help to acclimatise themselves. Those who have caused actual, intentional harm will find their new lives far from easy, especially when they develop a conscience. The phrase "an eye for an eye, a tooth for a tooth" is woefully misunderstood. It really applies to the Law of Cause and Effect and whatever harm we do to others, we will at some point in our evolution have to experience because that is how we learn.

I know of a case of a well-known film and TV actor who is now counselling bankers in the post mortem state. That is not to say that all bankers have difficulty, only those who made money their god. Money does not exist in their new abode so if they have not developed other interests they are miserable. For others, it is a joy because they can fulfil their wildest dreams without being constrained by a lack of finances.

All of the communicators in this book express the importance of unconditional love because it is eternal and the stuff of the Universe.

The initial impulse of this book has been waiting to be revealed for over thirty years but I lacked the courage to make the information public because the catalyst was a famous singer, Maria Callas. However, Helena Hawley, who was totally unknown to me, was contacted by Callas at the beginning of the new century in order to develop healing through sound and her books confirm my earlier experiences with this great soul.

To me, the truth is of the utmost importance, and this is my truth because it is my own experience. It is up to the reader to accept or reject it. I have played my part, now I hand it over to them.

Chapter One
Expansion

In 1973, my husband, Chris, and I along with Giles, our three-year-old son, moved into a late Victorian house in Harrow, north/west London. I had always been sensitive to the atmosphere and as soon as I stepped over the threshold of the empty house, I knew that it was for us. The room next to our bedroom seemed ideal for our son but he was restless at night and kept coming into our room. At first, I put this down to the unfamiliarity of new surroundings, then one day, as he was sitting on the floor playing with some bricks, he looked up and said, "You know, Mummy, you and Daddy and me, we've all been together before."
I didn't know what he meant but it seemed a strange thing for such a young child to say.

The disturbed nights continued then my twin nieces came to stay. They were three years older than Giles and they all had a lovely time together, dressing up and playing in the garden. After the girls returned home, Giles decided that he wanted to sleep in the guest room. We agreed to give it a try and after that, there were no more disturbed nights.

It was convenient for me to use the vacated bedroom as a sewing room and often, as I sat at my machine, I felt as if someone was standing beside me, watching me closely. Maybe our son was also aware of a presence but was too young to explain.

Apart from that room, we were delighted with the house which was light and bright and suited our lifestyle perfectly. I wasn't frightened of the presence because I was usually too busy concentrating on the work in hand to dwell on it. As well as being freelance singers working for various companies, my husband and I ran the Apollo Group of London with whom we produced operas and concerts around the UK. As I had first trained as a costume designer when I left school, I was responsible for the costumes for the shows as well as singing principal soprano roles.

I had had one or two odd experiences as a child but this house certainly triggered something unusual in me which developed over the next twenty years. Soon after we moved in we were given a black kitten by my sister, Mary, whom we named Tom. However, it didn't strike me at first that black cats have a rather mysterious reputation. My first inexplicable experience happened one evening a few weeks afterwards. My husband was at a rehearsal and my son was asleep so I went downstairs, made myself a cup of coffee, picked up a *Homes and Gardens* magazine and looked forward to enjoying a quiet evening. However, as I settled down, it seemed as if the top of my head opened up and I found myself way out in the Cosmos.

I should mention that I do not drink alcohol nor have I ever smoked or taken illegal substances because I would hate to be controlled by any kind of addiction. I was wide awake but I was in two places at once. One part of me was fully conscious on the sofa on earth but another aspect was in deep space. I could distantly see the earth and knew that my body was there, yet the planet was the size of a pinhead. I still retained my own personality so I wasn't afraid; just very curious. The only difference to my every day self was that I had the most unprecedented feeling of freedom, rather like a zoo animal having been taken from its cage and released into its natural habitat.

I could not see anyone but I knew I was not alone; a form of intelligence was telepathically communing with me. Then I had the impression of an invisible group. As I mentally queried who was 'talking' to me, a single eye appeared in space.[1] The entire experience was so lovely, that I did not want to return to Earth. I knew that my nearest and dearest were there but the sense of freedom was so overwhelming that I wanted to stay. However, suddenly the Cosmos dissolved and the walls of the sitting room closed in. I don't know how long the experience lasted but it was very real and as I had been fully conscious all the time I knew that it wasn't a dream. Even several decades later, the reality of it is still with me, whereas dreams are soon forgotten.

When my husband came home, I told him what had happened. Of course, he didn't understand it but was sympathetic as he realised that I had undergone a profound experience. I shall always be grateful to him because he was confident that I was a perfectly rational individual. However, he was challenged over the next two weeks because I kept saying that I felt trapped in my body and didn't see how I could manage to stay in it as I had experienced the most extraordinary, exhilarating freedom while out of it.

Some years later, a very good friend and colleague of ours had a psychic awakening which was the beginning of her spiritual journey, and healing became very important to her. However, her husband told friends that she had gone mad. Of course, like many people who have never had such experiences, he was frightened and eventually, as she could not give up her new knowledge, they divorced. The sad thing is that this isn't an isolated case. I have known other relationships break down because one of the parties was further along the spiritual path than the other.

Fortunately, my physical constriction gradually subsided and I began to feel comfortable in my body again. The benefit of my 'out of the world' excursion resulted in removing all fear of death because I now know that our consciousness exists independently of the body, and though at death the body is reduced to dust and ashes, our true selves depart to pastures new. Our body is like a car, enabling us to move around a physical planet but the driver is not the car. Another analogy

---

[1] Later I discovered that this feature is known as the Eye of Horus in ancient Egyptian art and is also called the All Seeing Eye of God.

is that of a computer with the brain as the hard drive and the mind as the software, which switches to another hard drive at death.

However, after our transition, we are not 'will of the wisps' but occupy a form which corresponds to the frequency of the new dimension. It would appear that the new body already surrounds the physical body but because it is on a faster vibration it is not seen with normal sight. Theosophists maintain that we have seven subtle bodies, each one finer than the previous one. It is rather like a static propeller, the form of which disappears when it is spinning.

We used to keep our radio tuned to BBC Radio Four but one day I switched on and found that it was on Radio Two. My husband must have been listening to cricket and had forgotten to change it back. As I got on with my ironing, I became interested in an interview with Lee Everett who was speaking about healing and spiritual matters. She was the wife of the TV comedian, Kenny Everett, and had opened a Healing Centre in Notting Hill.

Like many people in the UK, I grew up in the Christian tradition, going to church, Sunday school and singing in a children's choir at a local Methodist Chapel. I still live by the Christian ethics I was taught in childhood but all my adult life I have been a free thinker, interested in the philosophy of religion but not prepared to join a 'club' because I find orthodoxy too limiting and have no intention of being told what I can or cannot think or do. There have always been well-meaning people but on the whole religious history does not make pleasant reading. Even today terrible things are done in the name of religion which if in the realm of politics would cause riots on the streets. I have to admit that I am amazed that such vast numbers of people will put their personal power into the hands of religious dictators.

Few people choose a religion; they are born into it and don't give it much thought. Others may not feel at ease with the dogma but pay lip service because it is easier than rocking the boat, especially if they have been brought up in an ultra-orthodox community. Many people who lead busy lives hand over responsibility to the clergy because it is much easier to have a priest take them by the hand and lead them into Heaven rather than strike out on their own lonely pathway. That takes courage, thought, enquiry and commitment. Strangely enough, despite my undoubted reservations about religions in general, I have always had a strong spiritual sense and am certainly no atheist as I believe in a Supreme Being. However, I also believe that human beings have responsibility for the earth and that our free will is paramount. There is no dictatorship other than that we make for ourselves. Prayer can bring guidance but even the angels cannot force us to change and they weep at the sufferings we cause ourselves.

One day, my husband brought home a book entitled *Gildas Communicates*, channelled by Ruth White, which he had picked up in a second-hand book shop. I had never come across a book of channelled guidance before but I found it unusual and very interesting. Next, I discovered a book about St. Theresa of Avila, who, though a nun in a Roman Catholic convent in Spain several centuries ago had been a notable mystic at a time when such visionaries were usually regarded as heretics and severely punished. Nevertheless, she was allowed to remain in her convent and was later canonised.

I have always believed in prayer and had begun to ask for wisdom and guidance. I can't say that I expected anything, it just seemed a good thing to do but now I realise that I was actively being pointed in a spiritual direction. I booked an appointment with Lee Everett at her Healing Centre and found her warm and encouraging. She placed her hands on the crown of my head and the most amazing energy penetrated my skull and body right down to my toes, quite unlike anything I had ever felt before. She suggested that I go to her class to learn to meditate as a way of controlling psychic phenomena. I had two sessions then began to regularly meditate at home. I took to the practice very easily and each morning before breakfast I would sit quietly for half an hour in the bay window of our dining room overlooking our verdant little garden. As I sat with my eyes closed, vivid pictures would form on my inner screen, quite at random, like watching films. I had no idea what I was seeing but occasionally when settling down to TV in the evening there would be something that I had already seen that morning. The fact that it was quite out of time was uncanny and really set me thinking about the nature of reality.

By 1980, I had been a professional singer for fifteen years which, though enjoyable like all public careers, it had its stresses; requiring daily practise, study, learning, memorising, rehearsing and travelling, and I was feeling rather stale at that time. One night, returning to London with my tenor colleague, Brian, after singing the role of Rosina in *The Barber of Seville*, I told him how I felt and he suggested that I take a refresher course with his teacher, Mrs Campbell, at Wigmore Studios, in the West End of London.

The next day I made an appointment for a consultation but when the time came, I almost cancelled it. However, something urged me to go because I had nothing to lose but a lot to gain. Eugenia Campbell had studied in Italy in her youth; firstly with Jacopetti and then with the famous coloratura, Louisa Tetrazzini. She married a fellow singer, Donald Campbell, whom she met in Italy; then sang for several years as a coloratura soprano in Sweden. Later she returned to Britain where she took lessons with the famous Scottish soprano, Maggie Teyte, who had studied with the great late 19th-century Polish tenor, Jean de Rezke. Soon Mrs Campbell realised that teaching was her forte so gave up performing and set up a successful teaching practice. She was about seventy-seven when I met her but she was just as enthusiastic about singing as she had been in her youth. I was fortunate to be able to study with her even for a short period because her teaching stood me in good stead when I also became a singing teacher.

Shortly after beginning my lessons with Mrs Campbell, a conductor with whom I had previously worked, asked me to sing the role of Pamina in Mozart's *The Magic Flute*. I had performed the aria and the Papageno/Pamina duet many times in concert but had never learned the entire role. Most operas have sung recitative linking the big set pieces but this opera has spoken dialogue. It is a German form of opera known as Singspiel. Although opera singers have to be actors, this type of opera splits the performer into two, one learning the music and the text to which it is set, the other the dialogue.

As it was short notice, I offered to recommend other sopranos who already knew the role but Harry said he wanted me. I have always been a quick study so Mrs Campbell urged me to accept. I only had three days to learn it but I began to feel as if a female presence stood behind me whenever I picked up the score. Like all Mozart roles, it needs a fine technique, beauty of tone and great vocal poise. With the score under my arm, I travelled to Bath, where the performances were to take place, and stayed with married colleagues with whom I had sung many times. In fact, David was singing the principal tenor role of Tamino in this production. Their garden, high on a hill above Bath, was lovely and, as the weather was fine, I enjoyed studying the score in the sunshine. Each time I settled down, I was aware of an uncanny feeling of someone looking over my shoulder and coaching me. I didn't see anything but had an impulse to imbibe energy from a tree, not something I had ever previously thought of doing!

My first meeting with the other singers and the orchestra was at the dress rehearsal. I did not have time to feel nervous as I needed all my concentration on the music, dialogue and stage directions. The show went well and my husband and son came to see it and stayed for the weekend. At that time, the role proved to be a turning point for me because it restored my deep love of singing.

Chapter Two
An Ocean Less Travelled

In July 1982, my son, who was eleven years old, told me that a clairvoyant would be giving readings at his school fete the following weekend and he wanted me to see her. During the week he mentioned it several times but I thought he meant that it would be someone dressing up, having a bit of fun asking people to cross their palms with silver. I didn't really understand the term 'clairvoyant'. However, on leaving school, I studied at the Birmingham College of Art, I imagined that everyone saw pictures in their mind's eye but now I realise that I have been clairvoyant for most of my life.

Giles was a pupil at the Purcell School, a specialist music establishment, then situated at the top of Harrow Hill, in a wonderful, expansive garden, with a vista stretching as far as the 'pepper pots' of the old Wembley Stadium and beyond. It was nearing the end of the afternoon when Giles bounded over with his friend, Alex Heffes, (now a successful film composer) and asked if I had seen the lady. I laughed and told him not to be silly. Nevertheless, as he seemed so keen, I joined a little queue of people waiting outside a small tent.

On entering, I found a young, fair-haired, friendly Irish woman, who introduced herself as Christine Holohan; actually, I thought she said 'Christina'; consequently, this is what I have always called her. I suppose I had expected an old woman with a crystal ball, as in films, but she was only twenty-nine years old and there was no sign of a crystal ball.

After inviting me to sit down she asked me to give her something personal by which she could 'tune in'. Apparently, everything has its own frequency and objects retain the vibrations of the person involved, rather like film or sound on a magnetic tape. If the object is second hand it can cause confusion as it will also have the vibrations of previous owners.

I gave my engagement ring to Christine and after holding it for less than a minute she said that a lady was keen to contact me. She gave her name as Mary Callas and said she had been helping me with my singing. Christine had no knowledge of classical singing technique but the discarnate woman certainly knew a great deal about it, and through Christine, described music I was working on at that time; even focusing on particular phrases that I found difficult and moved on to then tell me how to deal with them. She mentioned my breaking off the breath before a high lying phrase just when I needed more support, not less. So, the helpful presence I intuited when I was learning Pamina was not a figment of my imagination.

It appeared that Christine was being used like a telephone linking two different dimensions. It was mind boggling. 'Mary' said she had literally died of a broken heart and could have had at least ten more years on earth. So, as she was very close to earth conditions, she was being allowed to help someone who had the same dedication to singing as she had. She had not lost her passion for singing and by helping me she would enhance her own spiritual development.

Unbelievable as it seemed, I suspected that this woman was the famous Maria Callas and thought that Christine had misheard her first name. However, I later discovered that she had been born in New York to Greek parents and was known as Mary at school and later by friends in Greece. Funnily enough, Christine, not being interested in classical music or opera, had never heard of Maria Callas.

To my shame, I now have to admit that I never liked Callas's very individual voice so whenever her recordings were played on radio I immediately switched off. I also fell for the press reports of a temperamental diva with a fiery temper and unpleasant personality. It must have been galling for her, famous as she was, trying to connect with someone who had no time for her. I loved beautiful voices and was particularly inspired by Joan Sutherland, Anneliese Rothenberger, Elisabeth Schwarzkopf, Sena Jurinac, Rita Streich, Lucia Popp and Lisa Della Casa. However, once I became aware of Maria as a delightful, intelligent woman, I began to listen to her recordings and found them a revelation. Admittedly, her voice was not to everyone's taste, though she had a formidable range and the ability to sing a wide variety of musical styles equally well. In addition, she was a consummate artist, fine musician and an intuitive, compelling actress. Her very soul sang and she could move audiences to tears with just the turn of a simple phrase.

Soon I found myself working with people, at home and abroad, who had known her professionally, such as Andy Anderson, house producer at the Royal Opera House, Covent Garden, who praised her unstintingly. Others also spoke of her professionalism, capacity for hard work and kindness to young singers. Through Jillian Skerry, my longest-serving pianist, I met Harold Rosenthal, the well-known opera critic who was devoted to Callas, not only as a formidable artist but as a personal friend and once at a party I met her biographer, Stelios Galatopoulos. We talked about her but I was too shy to tell him about her post mortem contact with Christine and me.

In 1992, when my son was studying at the Royal College of Music, Chris and I were allocated complimentary tickets for an end of term show at the Britten Theatre. When we went to collect them, we discovered that there had been a mix up so we were given alternative seats. Mine was next to Robert Sutherland, the pianist on Maria's last tour whom I recognised from a recent TV documentary about her. As he was on his own, I told him that I had enjoyed the programme and he told me about working with her and Giuseppe di Stephano on their last tour. Even at this late stage, I was too reticent to mention that I had known her psychically for the last ten years because I did not want him to think that he was sitting next to a crank. He said very nice things about Maria though he admitted that her voice had seriously deteriorated and her nerves were badly affected. He blamed her relationship with Aristotle Onassis as it had taken her away from the stage at the height of her powers. His jet set way of life was not conducive to the life of an opera singer which is one of intensive study, practise, constant work and sheer dedication.

Opera singers are vocal athletes and without frequent practise, the muscles weaken and the voice deteriorates. However, Robert emphasised Maria's courage as she had to face audiences who knew her from earlier recordings so inevitably realised that she was no longer the singer she had once been. He mentioned, in particular, a pianissimo high A in the final aria in *La Traviata,* when Violetta, the heroine, is dying. The note had never been one of Maria's best as it seemed to lie in an awkward slot for her and one evening she struck the note but it was an awful sound and she couldn't sustain it, yet consummate artist that she was, she immediately descended the octave on an exquisite glissando, thus turning a vocal disaster into a moving dramatic moment.

Going back to the day of the school fête in 1982, unknown to Christine, I was going to Munich the following week and when she began to describe places and buildings I would soon visit, I knew what she was talking about, though she didn't. I had visited the city and surrounding parts of Bavaria several times since 1967 and so recognised the descriptions she gave.

Just before our time was up she said that there was an elderly man who was waiting patiently to make contact. From her description, not just of his physical appearance but of his general manner, I recognised Pop, my father-in-law, who had died the previous year while we were in Salzburg. She also said that John was with him. This was his brother-in-law who had died three months later, while we were in Scotland. As may be imagined, this was a lot to take in, but when she said they had the Red Setter dog with them, it really seemed too much to swallow and I denied that they had ever had such a dog. When I told my husband, he confirmed that the dog was Paddy, the family pet when he was a toddler. Thus it seemed that animals, as well as people, were alive and well in the afterlife.

I have always been a seeker and as a child drove everyone crazy by my incessant questions. Now, I wanted to find out more about how Christine knew such things and as she had given me her card, I made an appointment for a private session when I returned to England.

Although the district where she lived was adjacent to mine, I do not drive, so had to take two buses and walk across a park, a main road then a couple of minor roads to reach her. It was very hot and I was wearing high heeled shoes and a smart suit with a pencil skirt, quite unsuitable on such a day. I rang her doorbell several times but there was no reply so I asked various neighbours if she had left a message. No one had any idea where she was but fortunately, there was a field at the side of the house and as usual, I had a book with me, so I sat and read for an hour. Finally, as there was still no sign of her; I gave up and began to walk back to the main road. There was a telephone box on the corner and something urged me to ring her but I knew that she wasn't in. However, the urge was so insistent that I rang her number and immediately, she answered the phone. She sounded breathless as she had, literally, just come through the front door. She had been to London and had a horrendous journey back due to a signals failure on the tube. However, at last, she was home and she asked me to return.

We had a refreshing cup of tea then she took my ring and quick as a flash, 'Mary' was back. She talked a good deal about her own life and struggles, particularly with the press, and of Aristotle Onassis, the man she had adored but who had treated her very badly, causing her world-wide humiliation when he married Jackie Kennedy, the widow of President John F. Kennedy. Onassis didn't want Maria to sing because he said he had enough money for both of them. He was insensitive to the fact that Maria's art was a vocation, not a job. However, to please him, she put her career into abeyance and joined the Jet Set, sailing the world on his magnificent yacht. She said that there had been a woman in public life who posed as her friend but ultimately betrayed her. Much later I suspected that this was the American, Elsa Maxwell, famed for throwing fabulous parties for socialites.

When Maria tried to resume her career, she found that her nerve had gone and her voice, though she tried to make up for lost time by practising assiduously, would never be the same again. Opera singers only use microphones when recording; otherwise, however large the theatre or concert hall, they have to produce their own power through breath support and the muscular strength of the diaphragm. This muscle is developed through years of training in order to project the sound. During the world tour with Giuseppe di Stephano, Maria was realistic enough to realise that it was too late to resurrect her career so went back to her beautiful apartment in Paris, where she lived with two servants and her little poodles. Here she became a virtual recluse, spending her time listening to her old recordings.

When Onassis's marriage to Jackie Kennedy proved less than idyllic, he resumed his relationship with Maria. Despite his shameful conduct, she told us that she still deeply loved him and when he died, she lost all interest in life. She said she had now met him again and though he had a lot to learn, she had forgiven him for all the hurt he had caused her. There had apparently been ill-feelings towards her by his children, Alexander and Christina. Alexander died young in an air crash and Christina soon followed him. Maria met them in the afterlife and wounds were healed.

She also told us that her mother left her father in New York and returned to Greece with her two daughters just as the Second World War was about to break out. Amazingly, during the war, Maria sang in opera though she was only a teenager. At the end of the war, she worked in an office dealing with military matters and became friendly with an English officer, though it was more a friendship than a romance. Many years later, this was confirmed by the officer who gave an interview to a national newspaper. Later, a book appeared about her time in Greece which referred to this man. At one sitting, however, she presented us with an enigma because she said that she had had a secret son. She never referred to it again so we were none the wiser.

Twenty-two years earlier in 1960, when I was working on the News staff at ATV in Birmingham, (a year before I went to London to study at the Guildhall School of Music and Drama) I was introduced to Sandor Gorlinsky, (Maria Callas's agent) and his wife, at the Coventry Festival and years later in a TV documentary about Maria, Mrs Gorlinsky said that she knew that Maria had become pregnant by Aristotle Onassis and though she would have liked a child, she allowed herself to be persuaded by him to have an abortion. Maybe when she left this world she met the soul who, had there been no abortion, would have been her son, which Christine sensed as being a secret.

I have since discovered that when our spiritual journey is about to begin, we are tested as to our commitment and tenacity. Well, my visit to Christine had been just such a test and I have to confess that in my younger days if something wasn't working, I would let go and do something easier. However, on this occasion, Christine had given me the chance to go back to see her. I later noticed that with the advent of Maria I developed more tenacity.

Chapter Three
Seeking Confirmation

I was now even more puzzled with the way things were developing so confided in Leon, a young colleague, who professed to be psychic and I asked him if he knew of a respected medium whom I could consult. Christine, though highly gifted, was a suburban girl and I wanted confirmation from someone who was eminent in their field. He advised me to book an appointment with Ivy Northage, at the College of Psychic Studies in South Kensington. I rang the college but was told that Mrs Northage was about to go to America on a lecture tour and was fully booked until she left. Normally, I would have accepted this, but instead, I asked to be notified if an appointment was cancelled. To my surprise, next morning I received a phone call informing me that Mrs Northage had an available session that afternoon. Fortunately, I was free so I set off for South Kensington without any idea of what a Psychic College would be like.

Though rather nervous, I was delighted to discover that it was a normal sort of educational establishment, occupying a typical 19th-century white stucco London house close to the Natural History Museum. The reception area was in the library and as I was early, I browsed among the books and was astounded to see what a vast array of literature there was on esoteric subjects. As an artist, colour has always been important to me so I was interested in a book on the subject by Marie Louise Lacey, little realising that I was shortly destined to study with her in the use of colour therapy.

Mrs Northage's room was at the end of a corridor and she stood at the open door watching me while I walked towards her. As we shook hands, she said quite casually, "Of course, you know you are psychic, don't you?"

I knew no such thing because I didn't then understand the definition of the term. My mother, my grandmother and her youngest son, John, whom I had never met, as he went to live in Australia before I was born, were all considered fey, which simply meant that they had a well-developed sixth sense.

Ivy invited me to sit down and asked me to give her something to psychometrise so I gave her the ring I had given Christine. At first, nothing happened and Ivy was puzzled as to why I was there. I, of course, didn't want to give anything away. It was obvious that I wasn't bereaved and didn't have any particular problems and when she asked what I expected of her, I simply said that I sought guidance. All was quiet for a while then suddenly I realised that Maria had made contact but she was playing with Ivy and wouldn't let her see her face. Instead, she held up a dark cloak but Ivy could see her wonderfully expressive hands and said that she was a very dramatic person. Unlike Christine, Ivy had some knowledge of singing as she had sung from childhood and her husband had been a good, amateur singer, who took part in Gilbert and Sullivan shows. When finally, the cloak was lifted, Ivy recognised that my 'singing coach' was none other than the famous Maria Callas.

I asked Ivy why she had picked me out but she said she had no idea. However, she must have telepathically consulted her guide, Chan, and he said that it was a past life connection. I felt as if my hair was standing on end. Suddenly, not only did I have to confront the reality of life after death, even for animals, but now had to face the possibility of reincarnation, which really pushed the boundaries. Maria said that in our immediate past lives, she and I had been sisters who were both singers but she had died young, so had not been able to help her little sister; now she was making up for lost time. Apparently, love is the guiding force at the root of everything, and though I was only just 'waking up', our love for each other in that life, and our eternal devotion to singing and music, had brought us together again. Strangely, I had forgotten that my three-year-old son had once told me that we had been together before.

Over the next few months, crumbs of information were dropped in my lap but I was certainly not given everything on a plate. I had to become researcher and detective to find out more. For a time scale, Maria set the scene by saying that we were on the Continent and Napoleon had fallen. I took that to mean his defeat in 1815 at the Battle of Waterloo but later I discovered that he died in 1821, the year her little sister was born.

From then on, everything happened thick and fast; books literally fell off shelves, which, when opened at random, would reveal something significant. At the same time, I became incredibly psychic as well as intuitive and visionary. It was like being on an uncharted ocean, not knowing the destination. However, I felt protected and guided.

I saw Christine regularly and each time, Maria would join us. She told us a lot about her personal life but also about her approach to her work. She was certainly one of the most dedicated artists there has ever been. Although opera has its leading lights, it requires teamwork as it is a combination of many arts; music, singing, drama, decor, acting etc. It was often said that Maria was difficult but she was only difficult if colleagues were not pulling their weight. Most people agreed that she was a perfectionist for whom nothing was too much trouble. She had no patience with lazy colleagues who traded on singing high notes but otherwise put in as little effort as possible. She said how infrequent it was for a production to work on every level but there was one opera in particular which pleased her immensely; that was the La Scala production of Donizetti's *Anna Bolena* with Maria in the title role. It was directed by Luchino Visconti and had the most amazing sets, costumes and lighting design as well as fine singers, chorus and orchestra. She also loved working with him on *La Sonnambula* by Bellini. For Callas's costumes, Visconti studied prints of Maria Malibran, a singer who had great success in the part of the heroine, Amina, at the beginning of the 19th-century. Callas had formerly been heavily overweight but was now very slim, and in her beautiful white costume with a garland of white roses on her swept-back black hair, she looked exactly like her 19th-century counterpart.

When Maria died, a miniature of Malibran was found beside her bed. As Callas, she believed that her last incarnation had been as Malibran and in that lifetime one of her best friends had been the Duke of Visconti, an ancestor of her director, Luchino Visconti. Thus, the whirligig of time goes around. She also told us that the composer, Gaetano Donizetti, whom she had known and worked with during her life as Malibran, had been her musical guide in her life as Callas.

I only had two years of lessons with Mrs Campbell because she died at the age of seventy-nine after a short illness. Maria then became my singing teacher with Christine as proxy. At first, I thought that Maria came purely because of our interest in singing and former family relationship but soon I realised that it was all part of my spiritual journey. I was being esoterically educated; particularly about the realities of reincarnation and the link between the material world and the unseen one. However, it was not one-sided because Maria said that helping me was necessary for her own spiritual development.

Our open channel attracted other people from her dimension, some of whom had also been very well known including Lord Mountbatten, who said that he and his wife, Edwina, were still concerned with Indian affairs. One name that Christine mentioned was unknown to me and seemed an odd one for her to have picked up. He was a German baritone named Heinrich Schlusnus, who had apparently been well known in Germany in the 1930s. Chris knew of him and said that he was a fine artist with a first-rate technique. Apparently, he was helping Chris and Giles when he became a baritone.

Each time Christine and I met at her house it was like a coffee morning with Maria popping in for a chat. Later, she brought others with her such as Ingrid Bergman, the Swedish film actress, who was charming and looked particularly beautiful because she positively shone in her attractive deep blue suit. The American film star, Grace Kelly, who had given up her career when she married Prince Ranier of Monaco, had also known Maria and she came to join her to see what her excursions to earth were all about.

Through my developing psychic ability, I was aware of 'visitors' in my house. One day I was passing through our hall when I heard, "Hello, Barbara" in a male voice with a Welsh lilt and saw my father-in-law sitting on the stairs. Next came Mary Garden, a singer from the past who wanted to re-live some of her performances with me particularly that of *Louise* by Charpentier as well as some of her other French roles, though they were not in my repertoire. However, she seemed delighted to know that I was aware of her.

I had found an easier way of getting to Christine's by tube and one day as I sat waiting for the train, I saw Maria sitting on a bench on the empty opposite platform. She smiled at me as if to say, 'yes, I shall be joining you and Christine soon'. Sure enough, when we settled down with our coffee, there she was.

Several actors made contact with me, possibly because from my early childhood, I loved the theatre. My father bought a TV set in 1953 and I enjoyed the plays that were broadcast live. The standard of drama was high, with plays by J. B. Priestley, George Bernard Shaw, J. M. Barry, Clemence Dane, Terence Rattigan, Pinero, Pirandello and Shakespeare, of course. In addition to up and coming young actors, I remember classical actors such as Sir Donald Wolfit and Robert Atkins, who reflected an older style of performance. The pool of younger actors included Richard Bebb, William Russell, Alan Badel, Brian Forbes, Andree Melly, Rosalie Crutchley and Andrew Osborne, an actor with a most mellifluous voice who soon gave up acting to become a director. His performance as Alexander the Great still resonates with me and it is a pity that it is now lost to posterity. I took interest even in the smallest bit-part players and when I see them in old films I can still recall their names. Some, of course, went on to very successful careers on stage and screen.

Psychically, I was particularly aware of Roger Livesey, who was looking after actors who had just gone over, including Sir Ralph Richardson, whom I found very humorous. I could see him walking on the terrace of a house and I asked if I should contact Lady Richardson and tell her he was alright.

"Oh, don't do that, dear girl," he said, "you'd frighten the life out of her." John Gregson was another communicator but he was disgruntled because he felt he should have had a more outstanding career. He was successful in British films, particularly that of *Genevieve*, but he had wanted to be an important international star.

While I was having an enjoyable time with my psychic gifts, Christine was being challenged in a more dramatic and sinister way. One day at her house, I could see that she was disturbed and she asked if I was aware of anything frightening. I had to admit that everything seemed fine to me. Christine shared the house with her sister, Mary and Mary's teenage son and they always greeted me as a family friend. After a cup of tea and a chat, we would go into another room; Christine would tune in and Maria would join us. It was all very pleasant and Christine would pick up information for my family as well as receiving Maria's input. One day she referred to my husband as Ivan. I told her she had got his name wrong. Of course, she knew that it was Chris but seemed surprised when I queried the name Ivan and she asked if he was playing a character by that name. I assured her that he wasn't. We didn't linger on it as there was a lot of other stuff coming through but over ten years later I discovered that it was relevant and a new avenue of research opened up.

Christine said that at night she was pestered by a girl named Jacquie who said she had been murdered in a neighbouring district. Christine had little time or inclination for reading newspapers but she may have heard about the crime when out shopping. However, it meant little to her until Jacquie appeared at the foot of her bed. She implored Christine to help her and gave her no peace until she agreed to go to the police. Jacquie told her that the killer was a friend of her boyfriend and gave his peculiar nickname. She said he had murdered her for her jewellery. She was intent on having him brought to justice and must have looked for someone in the vicinity with the relevant ability to move between worlds; Christine proved to be that person.

Although she had never been in contact with the police, Christine finally went to her local police station and told them what she knew. It was not until almost two decades later when one of the detectives had retired that she learned just how accurate she had been. Out of more than a hundred clues, she was only wrong on one. She thought that it happened on a Saturday night because at first Jacquie had been preparing to go out, but feeling unwell, she decided to stay in. Actually, it was a Friday night. The police were somewhat wary because Christine knew so much and they wondered if she had had anything to do with the murder. However, all things considered, they gave her the benefit of the doubt, thanked her for her trouble and, as far as she was concerned, that was that.

I was well aware of the effect it had on Christine. She is an optimistic, upbeat, cheerful person but Jacquie had put her through the agony of her death throes in order to make her understand how it had happened. Eighteen years later, Christine was told that a former suspect had been apprehended. He had moved to another part of the country several years before, but because the case was not closed, the police had kept an item of his clothing. Forensics had moved on in the intervening years so when he was accused of a driving offence, there was DNA evidence with which to charge him. He was tried, convicted and sentenced to a lengthy period in prison. The writer, Vera McHugh, collaborated with Christine on a book about the case which was first published in Ireland by Maverick House Press in 2006 under the title, *A Voice from the Grave*, and then in 2011, it was re-issued by the Ebury Press as *A Whisper from an Angel*.

Christine is a very honest person but unfortunately, members of the murdered girl's family made her life unpleasant by maintaining that she had made money out of the murder. Nothing could be further from the truth because unless a writer is well known, it is very difficult to make money from writing and Christine would have been lucky to cover her travel expenses incurred in promoting the book.

It is alleged that someone with Christine's extraordinary gift can transfer energy to another person via a talisman and I think that was what was happening to me, because every time Christine held my ring, some of her psychic energy must have been transferred to me and that was why my psychic abilities were developing at such a fast rate.

Chapter Four
A New Line of Study

It was as though I had two lives; one as a professional singer and one as a spiritual adventurer. Looking back it amazes me that I was able to cram so much into just twenty-four hours a day. Of course, I also had to sleep but it appeared that my consciousness operated at that time too. In order to understand more, I joined the College of Psychic Studies and frequently attended the Tuesday lectures (where I especially enjoyed the channelled talks by Ivy Northage and her guide Chan) as well as weekend workshops and six-week courses. I also read widely and studied with fascinating teachers such as Marie Louise Lacey, Elizabeth Farrell and Robin Winbow. I also met Tony Neate, a founding member of the Atlanteans of Runnings Park and his wife, Ann, a former singer; Brenda Marshall, the President and the writer Rosamund Lehmann, the Vice President. Fellow students were a fascinating bunch and included the *Carry On* film actress Fenella Fielding (who used a pseudonym) and her friend, the outspoken journalist Molly Parkin. I also made several personal friends including Bridget Hickey, a textile designer who went on to run marathons when she retired; Lawrence French, a retired publisher who was then a lay brother at Charterhouse in the City of London and Jane Hirst, a former nurse and later Jungian who settled in France in order to explore past lives. Jillian Skerry and I have visited Jane several times and have fallen in love with her small medieval village in a sweeping hilly countryside, which is a wonderful backdrop for our paintings.

I also stayed several times at the Seeker's Trust at Addington Park, a hamlet near Maidstone, where the local pub is named *The Angel*. It was here that I first heard Peter Dawkins' lecture and met his wife, Sarah. Peter is an architect, writer, expert on the Shakespearean plays and extraordinary visionary, who lectures around the world, often with Sarah. He founded the *Gatekeeper* and *Francis Bacon Research Trusts* and the *Zoence Academy* where the science of life, based on Ancient Wisdom, is taught. I was originally a member of the *Gatekeeper Trust* and am now a Friend of the *Francis Bacon Research Trust*.

From time to time the *Gatekeeper Trust* arranges a Pilgrim's weekend, led by Peter and Sarah and one year, in November, I went with them to Gaunt's House in Dorset. On the Sunday morning, we went to Knowlton Church, a ruined Norman edifice built on a Neolithic henge. We explored the site then Peter suggested that our group of forty should go into the nave of the church and do some toning. Each person chooses and sustains a note then changes it at will. At first, it is very discordant but then the individuals appear to become a vocal orchestra and intuitively beautiful harmonies result. I was completely immersed in the sound and so closed my eyes and to my astonishment, I saw the most extraordinary geometric shapes made of coloured light emanating from the sounds. They soared beyond the ruined walls and floated endlessly over the landscape. Another phenomenon is the fact that even though there is a large group of people involved, they all stop at exactly the same time without any direction from an outside source. Maybe it is a kind of collective morphic resonance, the kind of thing scientist, Rupert Sheldrake hypothesises about migrating birds.

I have a theory that the ancients used this practice as part of a science of sound in order to generate energy. It is possible that we will develop it and use it in the future as part of a healing process; probably alongside orthodox doctors to speed up recovery.

I already knew Andrew, a young psychiatrist, from other trips and we were joined by Alice, a newcomer to *Gatekeepers*. When we got back to Gaunt's House, the three of us had coffee together and though I am usually very reticent about disclosing my experiences on other levels, I told my companions what I had seen. Quite casually, Alice confided that she had seen the same thing. After so many years such experiences are a natural part of life to me but I realise that it is not usually so for others.

I always ask my inner guidance to let me know when to speak and when to stay silent and there are people who have known me for decades who have no idea about the spiritual aspect of my life. However, I am not a Spiritualist as that is a religion and I do not adhere to any organised religion. As I have waited for over thirty years to publish this book, no one could say that I rushed in unthinkingly. The experience at Knowlton Church was a wonderful confirmation that on another frequency, sound is visual as well as auditory and affects matter. Although Alice's father was a bishop, at that time she was very much into New Age thinking. Later, she and Andrew married and had a son then, to everyone's surprise, she became an ordained vicar.

Although over the years my innate faith has been strengthened, the knowledge has taken me ever further away from dogmatic religion while others become more orthodox in their beliefs which shows that each person has an individual path to tread. Thus, there is no right or wrong way, only what is fundamentally true for that person.

The 19th-century singer, Pauline Viardot Garcia, the subject of my two-volume biography, was a great friend of the composer, Franz Liszt and both of them had a strong spiritual sense but like me, Pauline shunned orthodoxy while, in his later years, Liszt became an abbé in the Roman Catholic Church. As lifelong friends, they were fond of each other but had to agree to differ when it came to religion. We could all learn from them because religion has always been a bone of contention, generating conflicts even though, ironically, we are all aiming for the same destination even if the routes are many and varied.

The strange thing is that I now know that I have been a Roman Catholic in several past incarnations and was a high ranking cleric in the 16th-century. Now, it seems that I have reached a stage where I have to continue my journey without that kind of crutch.

One of the offshoots of my inner experiences was the development of healing energy and absent healing. I also discovered the Dr Edward Bach Flower Remedies, which I frequently use for my family and recommend to everyone. Dr Bach was a highly qualified orthodox doctor and Harley Street consultant but he decided that it was essential to treat the patient not just the symptoms of a disease or illness. He gave up his practice and went into the countryside because he said that nature had provided so much for us, all we had to do was discover it. From his researches, he devised the Flower Remedies. He said that the vast majority of illnesses are caused by stress. However, every patient is an individual and no two individuals react in the same way to life's stresses and strains.

His remedies are prepared by infusing flowers or pieces of bark from a tree in pure water, left in the sun for three hours on a hot, clear day. The flowers are then drained off and a small amount of brandy or cider vinegar is added to the water to avoid stagnation. This becomes the stock remedy and two drops are added to a phial of spa water. That becomes the treatment and aids the body's own healing mechanism with no side effects. There are thirty-eight remedies, five for different types of fear and two for depression. The thirty-ninth remedy is called the Rescue Remedy because it saved the life of a fisherman who had been swept overboard. Dr Bach was walking along the beach at Cromer and saw the unconscious man on a stretcher, he realised that he had a phial with three remedies in his pocket so he dripped some onto the man's lips and in a short time he gained consciousness and asked for a cigarette. Dr Bach added two further remedies and called it the Rescue Remedy. There are also sprays now and a cream. In 2013, I took the foundation course and received my Stage One certificate, this was followed by my taking Stage Two and Three at Dr Bach's former home, now the Bach Centre in Sotwell in Oxfordshire. However, I have never practised healing professionally or used any of my psychic gifts commercially; though I am always willing to help if asked and send absent healing to those on my list during my meditation sessions each day.

Despite all the esoteric material with which I had to deal, I continued my busy singing career which included work abroad. In addition, in 1985, I was guided to set up a course in Stress and Self Awareness; two sessions a week at a local Further Education College. I was a pioneer in those days because what I taught was considered avantgarde, although such subjects have now entered the mainstream. There were fine, sound teachers at the College of Psychic Studies and I gained a great deal of knowledge from them. However, after five years, I left my local college as I had begun to teach singing privately. Nevertheless, the classes provided a nucleus of students who formed a meditation group at my home on Thursday evenings.

I was also helped by Valerie, a soprano colleague of my husband's, who described herself as a 'Cosmic Mrs Mop'. Until I met Christine, I had never met anyone like Valerie. She was a consummate professional with whom Chris and Marian, a mezzo friend and colleague, had worked for several years. I was offered the role of Abigail in 'Nabucco' with Chris in the title role but I knew that it was not right for my voice. However, Valerie had been successful in such roles so I recommended her and she rose splendidly to the challenge.

I first met her some years before I met Christine when Marian invited Chris, me and Valerie to dinner. I found her conversation absolutely riveting because she spoke of happenings on the earth some 30,000 years ago and my appetite was whetted. From childhood, I had been fascinated by pre-history and doubted many of the accepted hypotheses conceived by 'experts'. She also revealed that she was psychic and spoke of experiences that were quite habitual to her.

After meeting Christine, I got in touch with Valerie and told her what was happening to me. She treated my revelation about Maria as if it was the most normal thing in the world and said that she was in touch with Kathleen Ferrier, a mezzo/contralto whom everyone had loved, not just for her voice, but because she was a very special person; spiritually radiant but with an earthy sense of humour. Sadly, she died from cancer at the age of 41. Thus, like Maria, she was helping those still on earth. Valerie said that as well as being involved with music, healing was a large part of Kathleen's remit. Years later this was confirmed by another source. [2]

---

[2] Helena Hawley

Chapter Five
Maria Is Upset

Just after meeting Valerie, we were on tour in Scotland and after a concert at Forfar, Chris, Jill and I were given hospitality by a man named Norman and his wife. He was a retired principal of a college and both were on the concert committee. They arrived back home while we were changing at the theatre and when Norman opened the door to us, as he shook hands, he said to me, "I knew you were coming."

I thought that was a strange thing to say because we had been invited to supper and were to stay the night. At some point, Norman said that he and I were kindred spirits and began to talk to me about the Cathars, an early medieval heretical group in southern France.

Like most people, I had never heard of them until the previous week when there had been a documentary about them on TV though I didn't have a chance to see the whole programme as I was called away to the telephone. However, Norman was fascinated by the film as he had already come across a book by Dr Arthur Guirdham, who alleged that a group of his patients in the West Country believed that they were reincarnated Cathars, having previously been horrendously done to death by agents of the Roman Catholic Church. One woman had scars on her present body indicative of having been burned at the stake and she was able to explain to Dr Guirdham just what it was like. All references to Cathars had been expunged from public records by the Church so it was not until fairly recently that scholars had begun to investigate them in the Vatican library.

It was interesting hearing about them but then the conversation moved on to other things. As we were about to go to bed, Norman handed me an illustrated book about the work on archetypes by the philosopher and psychoanalyst, Carl Gustav Jung. I had heard of Sigmund Freud but not Jung and had no idea what archetypes were. However, over the next few years, I became aware of them in my inner world so am grateful to Norman for introducing them to me as, otherwise, I would have been all at sea.

Looking back, I know that people such as Norman, Valerie, Christine, Ivy Northage, Lawrence French and Peter Dawkins, were placed on my path as signposts and I am deeply grateful because they helped me to keep my feet on the ground, even when my head was in the air. Fortunately, I am a pragmatic, everyday kind of person but I can imagine that some people, undergoing similar experiences without such support would be hard-pressed to keep their equilibrium.

After his wife died, Norman moved to Cambridge so I often saw him when staying with Jillian because she taught at the University. He was a wise old boy and he was able to assure me that though I felt that I was on an uncharted ocean, other mariners had sailed it from time immemorial. Norman died in the late 1980s but even though I often thought of him, I never received a communication. However, I am now sure that he was an initiate who was on earth to shine a light for beginners like me who had just begun their spiritual journey.

From 1985, I was a conscious channel of esoteric material and received communications from several people who had made their transition to other dimensions. Often it happened in meditation or dreams. I began to keep notebooks but then wrote down the telepathic messages. It was not automatic writing but mind to mind contact, rather like taking dictation very fast, the words floating along on a sort of conveyor belt. I could not mentally query anything because the conveyor belt would go on without me. I learned to simply write and it was so fluid that there were no crossings out or interruptions, even in a long screed. Though I wrote in longhand, it looked as if I was writing shorthand.

I owe so much to Maria and Christine and realise now that singing was just the tool that Maria used to enable me to understand that human beings are multidimensional and what we normally regard as reality is just the tip of the iceberg.

Whenever Christine, Maria and I got together, the atmosphere was light and jovial but one day Maria seemed very anxious. The crux of the matter was that Chris had recently brought home a book by Maria's ex-husband, Giovanni Battista Meneghini, entitled *My Wife, Maria Callas*. It had first been published in Italian in 1980 but Chris had picked up a 1981 English edition. If he found himself with time to kill between rehearsals or performances he would browse in book shops. He was tickled pink to find the Meneghini book and naturally, we both looked forward to reading it in order to find out more about Maria and see if it confirmed what she had told us. However, Maria said that she didn't want us to read it because it was full of lies.

Of course, our curiosity got the better of us and I found that Meneghini did not attempt to blacken her character. When they married, she was twenty-six and he was a successful businessman in his fifties who put aside his own business interests in order to manage her career. It was not all plain sailing at the beginning but with his money and influence, important doors began to open and her career was launched in Italy. The marriage was naturally advantageous to her but, from her letters, she did seem genuinely fond of her husband and he admitted that he was in love with her. However, at that time she was overweight and physically quite unlike the slim, elegant Callas she became.

Meneghini's management was not always to her advantage because often he fell out with opera house administrators then the press blamed Callas for being temperamental. There was a lot of misunderstanding by the press regarding the demanding life of an international opera singer of her calibre and this soured her relationship with the media.

We soon realised that what she didn't want us to read about was her uncharacteristic behaviour when she first began the affair with Onassis. He had been very insistent with his invitation for her and her husband to join a cruise on his yacht with several luminaries, including Sir Winston Churchill and his wife. Maria had not been at all keen to go but during the cruise, Onassis, whose wife was on board, made such a play for Maria that he completely turned her head. She was a very moral woman who had always taken her marriage vows seriously and the behaviour of some of the guests on the yacht surprised her.

Since her youth her life had been dedicated to music; indeed she saw herself as a priestess of music. Now, for the first time in her life, she was sexually aroused and she found it unbelievably exhilarating. Onassis was sturdy and shorter in stature than Callas and not at all good looking but he was an experienced and expert lover and Maria found him irresistible. Her husband had always been a father figure to her, affectionate but unexciting. With the advent of Onassis, the passion, which up to now had only been released on stage, took her over so completely that she became totally reckless.

The upshot was that Tina Onassis divorced her husband and Maria and Meneghini's marriage was, after great difficulty, finally annulled. The passion which now held Maria in thrall was a kind of madness which would not only destroy her career and her peace of mind but would ultimately break her heart.

No wonder she didn't want us to read the book. Of course, she had already told Christine and me that she had lost interest in life when the man she loved died and admitted that she died from a broken heart. We realised that although she was devoted to him, he had treated her badly but we had not known any details about the start of the affair or of Maria's subsequent treatment of her husband.

It didn't make us think any the less of her; merely that, despite her legendary status in the realm of opera, she was as subject to temptations as anyone else. We were sad to think that her lover was unworthy of her and that in the end, her sacrifice brought her nothing but unhappiness.

Her attitude to this book took us by surprise because we assumed that she had overcome earthly regrets. However, it reminded her of her own frailty and it appears that even after death she had enough ego left to resent the fact that it could damage her posthumous reputation. She was *La Divina*, a legend in her own lifetime, and she was still jealous of her hard-earned fame. It certainly made us realise that if we depart this life with regrets or unfinished business, we can suffer the pangs of conscience in the afterlife.

Chapter Six
The Curtain Dissolves

In 1986 my father had a massive heart attack but made an unexpected recovery. Previously, he had recovered from a severe bout of Pleurisy and a massively severe coronary infarction which was almost fatal. Afterwards, he had an operation for bowel cancer which was also touch and go. He also lost his sight. After the second heart attack, he lived for another four months which were the most contented of his life. He and my mother who, though married for fifty years were frequently sparring partners, enjoyed true peace and compatibility for his remaining months.

One morning, he said he was tired so my mother told him to stay in bed. Michaela, his granddaughter, took his lunch upstairs then went to get him a cup of tea. She was not away long but in the meantime, he quietly slipped away. My sister, Mary, rang me in Harrow and immediately, I caught a train to Birmingham. Fortunately, it was quiet in the carriage and as I was not in the mood for reading, I sat with my eyes closed, thinking of all that had to be done to help my mother when I arrived. There was a stop at Rugby and as the train resumed its journey, though my eyes were closed, I saw my father's face as if on an inner screen. I mentally asked if he could see me and he said he could. This was strange as he was registered blind.

He began to tell me what had happened and it was like watching a film. He said he had felt weary and while trying to eat his lunch found himself out of his body. There was an 'old boy' with him (Dad was 77 himself) who said, "Let's get out of here," and they floated through the wall!

I still had my eyes closed but I saw a lot of soldiers gathering around Dad; he also saw a neighbour from years back and said, "Sorry, I have to go now duck," and suddenly my screen went blank.[3]

Years later, I had another strange experience at Rugby and wonder if there is something in that area that opens up a portal. It is not far from Daventry where there are a lot of radio masts and I believe an atomic clock is in the vicinity. I

---

[3] Dad had been with the British Expeditionary Force in Normandy at the beginning of the war and as he was a singer, entertained the troops there. Everyone was frightened of the future and what it might bring and Dad's singing gave them heart and enjoyment at a difficult time. Now they wanted to thank him.

It was strange though that the first people who greeted him were relative strangers and that the first person he knew was a neighbour rather than a member of his family.

know nothing about electricity, electronics or science but I have often thought that some kind of radio waves may be responsible for psychic experiences. However, I don't think that orthodox science has found a link yet.

When I arrived home, my sisters and nieces were still in a state of shock, though my mother was very calm as she planned what to do next. I told them that I had been in touch with Dad on the train but they didn't take in what I was saying. After a couple of days, I had to go home as I had commitments. I returned with my family for the funeral and the night before I felt a strong presence and had the feeling that Dad would like me to say a few words at the service. I picked up a pen and paper and began to write but it felt as if I was taking dictation. At the ceremony, I read the piece very calmly without a tear or nerves and everyone was amazed that I was able to do so without becoming emotional.

EPITAPH

On behalf of our family, I'd like to give thanks for Dad's life. He loved children and did all he could to make our childhood happy. I was a very curious child, always asking questions, yet he was never short of an answer and his knowledge fascinated me.

His ready wit and sense of humour delighted all who knew him and he could laugh at himself too. Many were his talents, a gifted singer and with journalistic abilities, yet life deprived him of opportunities and he knew frustration. However, in my mother, he had a tower of strength and despite not always seeing eye-to-eye with her, there was a deep bond of affection between them. They weathered fifty years together, growing ever closer at the end.

Dad would be surprised to hear me call him a man of courage but so he was. The last twenty years of his life brought much serious illness and blindness, yet he bore it with fortitude. He was very afraid of death and earlier this year experienced what I can only call 'the dark night of the soul', however, through an inner faith, he came into the light.

His last night on earth was a wonderful dispensation. His grandson, Steven, said the atmosphere in the house was very special. Dad felt a great sense of peace and told my mother he'd had a beautiful evening. He slept well but the 'messenger' was drawing close and the end came so easily and gently the following day.

In his last years, he derived a lot of enjoyment from BBC Radio FM. It was his lifeline and he was delighted to know several of the presenters personally. He was so thankful to still have his unimpaired hearing.

We shall remember him for his love for us and for his singing which came from the heart and for his humour which uplifted many people. His family know that he hasn't gone far but is only a thought away.

After Christmas, my sister, Mary, brought my mother to stay with me. One morning, Mum was in the study with me and Mary was in the kitchen preparing food. I was writing a shopping list and Mum was reading when a photo of Dad in a funny hat fell out of my notebook. I showed it to Mum and we laughed because he looked so comical; then she went back to her magazine and I to my list. I had the impression that someone was standing beside me and I suspected that it was Dad as we had been speaking about him. I had a pen in my hand and suddenly had the thought of mentally asking Dad if he could write through me. He had always been a keen and frequent letter writer but I felt him hesitate as if wondering if he really could. Telepathically, I told him to have a go and put my pen to the paper. The following is what came through.

DAD'S FIRST 'LETTER'

16th, February 1987

Dorothy love,

I haven't gone far away, you know. I'm often just over your shoulder. I like to sit with you when you're quiet. It's nice when the others go out because I have you to myself. Even if you don't know I'm there, I like to know you're thinking of me. But I don't want you to be sad because you did all you could for me and now I realise what an old buffer I could be, to put it mildly. I often took it out on you when I was frustrated and mad with myself. I let myself down and then blamed you. Now I ask your forgiveness and want to tell you all you mean to me. I wish I could have expressed it years ago. I think of all the time I wasted and am truly ashamed.

However, I have to look on the bright side; if I allow all those old thoughts to take me over, I'm done for. There is a lot of light and colour and loveliness (on his side) and if we can only stay with that we inhabit a beautiful world. I wish I could show you some of the wonders of it. Perhaps I'll be able to in your dreams.

We did make a lot of wonderful music together, didn't we? It is the glory of our lives. I can now see the pictures and patterns of colour that music made as well as the enjoyment we gave to others. I can now actually feel their emotions and I am surprised at the impact we had. We are a wonderful couple, partnership you know, and it can go on. There really isn't any death. Barb was quite right. I wish I'd listened to her more. What a pity people like her are so often treated as cranks. Do try to understand what she tells you and read more because it will mean so much to you and will make such a difference when you come over here. I'll be waiting for you with open arms and things will be so different. All the years we missed out on through our pigheadedness will be made up for. I still have a lot of lessons to learn but I am a much humbler person now than the one you knew. I gasp at my old arrogance and am so ashamed but believe me, I'll make up for it, only do say you forgive me and that you will want to be with me when you come over. I love being around the family. I'll do all I can from my side to make sure you're all alright and not worried about money. Trust that you will be provided for.

I think Barb's power is running down and I don't want to overtire her. Remember I'm only a thought away. Call on me at any time. We can talk over anything that bothers you. I do love you so dearly, please believe that and I thank you from the bottom of my heart for everything.

I'll try to contact you tonight but even if no one actually picks up my thought, do know I shall be in the room with you all. I like Barb's people; they're wonderful fun and such good, loving souls[4]. Till tonight; all my deepest love, Albert.

My mother and sister returned home after a few days, but having found a 'cosmic phone', Dad continued to communicate with me.

27th February 1987

Dear Barb,

So glad to talk with you again. Thanks a thousand for providing the link. Your Mum and I are closer now than we've ever been. Daft, isn't it to think it took death to bring us so closely together.

I was with you last night (in the meditation and healing session). I really enjoyed myself. I wish you could have seen it from my side – talk about a picture. No artist on earth could capture such beauty. You're doing a grand job, never doubt that and don't be despondent when things don't work out. You give people the opportunity to learn; it's not your fault if they don't accept it. Just keep on going because it's lovely from your side and ours. You think you are helping the people around you but you also help those on my side. Many souls gather close when you have your classes because the colour and sound you all send out provide a great healing power and many who could not stand the more powerful vibrations on our side are enabled to draw benefit from your efforts.

I have been around a lot and it gladdens my heart when I am invited to join in but so far I haven't been able to speak to them[5] – only to try to impress their thoughts. Because you are trained you are able to assist me as others cannot. But I do wish them to go on welcoming me if only to sit with them a while and intermingle with their auras. There is much more I can do to help them than I ever could on earth and in a more meaningful way – not just materially but in seeing further than they do, guiding them and getting healing to them.

There are all sorts of help over here; I am just coming to realise. All you have to do is ask. I was a bit reserved at first. Nice as it was to see old friends, I didn't feel I fitted anywhere in particular and have spent most of my time coming home. The old boy[6] has been most patient and has let me find my feet. Now I see just how helpful I can really be and must get myself trained, and really start a learning programme. I received the thought you sent out that we could work together but didn't know what you meant. Now I am beginning to see all sorts of possibilities and will be like a foreign correspondent. Of course, I haven't ventured far afield yet but I'll take every opportunity to progress and you've given me great purpose. I now have the incentive to learn and my existence has a purpose as never before.

---

[4] My meditation group in Harrow
[5] His daughters and granddaughters
[6] Possibly a guide

Yes, do let's try to write a book together. We must do all we can to relieve ignorance and bigotry.

I see you have to go now; Yes, I really do see. Give my love to Chris and Giles and lots of kisses and hugs to your Mum and all the others. Tell Mary she isn't forgotten and please not to be afraid. I love her more than ever – as I do all of you. Love to Jill too. I look forward to the rehearsal.[7]

---

[7] Mid-morning, Barbara and her pianist Jillian Skerry were due to begin a rehearsal for a recital.

Chapter Seven
A Regular Correspondence

1st March 1987

What a long time it took you to get going today. I've been waiting to make contact. I missed you writing yesterday. It's the most important link I've got. I feel I've come home. Sorry about the girls not accepting[8] – nothing you can do at present; it's beyond them. Never mind, just keep going, it's all you can do. You don't need me to tell you how awkward people can be – only a short time ago I was the same.

Do understand I haven't gone far yet. I know in time I'll have to move on but so far I'm still very tied to my family. I realise they are the strongest love links I have – no one on this side means as much to me as my own immediate family. People are kind but I'm not yet ready to let go. If I can work with you it will help me too and I'm being allowed to form this link with you, not just because we're family but because the work of enlightening people is the most important thing going forward in the world today. They must learn there is no death – everything else will then take its place and so much that is a mystery will open up to them.

First of all, I have to get my vibes right. I was so upset when I found out what had happened to me. I felt so well and happy at first but suddenly it dawned on me that I'd lost my family. Well, you must realise how panicky I felt when I could see them and was so close and they couldn't see me. It was like banging on a plate glass window. I could see out but nobody could see in. I simply couldn't make anybody hear. I felt emotionally overcome and so alone. I knew there were people on my side concerned about me; there were lots I had known and liked but the links weren't firm enough. It was my family I wanted, particularly your mum. Boy, did I miss her and it was then that I realised just how much I owed her and how much she'd put up with. My heart was fit to burst when I saw how I'd affected her at times. The old boy[9] was very patient. He didn't harass me but let me see the pictures of my life and all the chances I'd missed. It is something we all have to go through and it hurts like hell. I wasn't concerned with the good times but only saw and felt all I'd misused and lost out on. Your mum is a saint, you know. Oh, I know she has her faults like anybody else but they're only minor ones. She has borne so much so courageously and

---

[8] The reality of the contact with him.
[9] His guide

never lost her will to help all those in trouble. I was a millstone around her neck. What a pillock I was. We should have laughed more and quarrelled less. Yes, the last months were better; I'd suffered[10] and come to my senses but it was too late and I still have to come to terms with the waste. I really will make it up to her when she comes here, believe me.

I'm obsessed with the way I treated her. She was like the rock of ages – such strength but I was a weak chicken and no support to her at all; in fact, I made things worse. Oh, the shame of it. The old boy says I will forgive myself in time but at present that's hard to believe. I ask her forgiveness and want her to know my love for her is overwhelming me. I love you all but at present all my thoughts are with your Mum. I don't want her to be unhappy; she has nothing to blame herself for. I'm sorry if I sound full of self-pity and miserable but believe me, it shakes you rigid to see the results of your mistakes. I was so pigheaded. No wonder I went physically blind – I just wouldn't see – I might have lived my whole life with my head in a plastic bag for all the perception I had. I'm not surprised you all ganged up on me at times – I deserved it.[11]

We really do judge ourselves more harshly than anyone else would. I have to clear so much rubbish before I can really plan ahead but even my earlier experiences will help you, Barb, in this book you plan. If it helps others to live a godlier life then it is all worth it. It's the only thing that keeps me buoyant at present. I am not yet aware of any Heavenly figures, being only on the lower rungs of the ladder. Everybody I've met so far is very kind and understanding, yet I am not aware of crowds of people, only those who have been in my own life. Of course, they all have their own work and lives to live. There will be lots of opportunities for me in the future, once I have cleared my backlog and can then have a choice of the way I want to live and work. I would like to help in scientific discoveries for the future.

I never did any science on earth but I am fascinated by new discoveries and would like to be a part of them. Early days, yet I still have so much to think about on a personal level.

I asked him if he had discovered anything about the golden arrows and he said, [12] I asked the old boy who said it was a call. I'd been given every chance to come to my senses but I'd left it so late and was still in so much darkness (ignorance). The only way they could reach me was to do this and unfortunately, I had to be brought to my knees and suffer emotionally as well as physically. I'd grown a hard shell to physical suffering – I learned to put up with it when really I should have been asking what had caused it and realised that much of it came

---

[10] In order to give his wife a rest; he went into a care home for a few weeks.

[11] He was being incredibly hard on himself because he was a decent husband, who drank little, did not gamble or womanise, He was always in work but was not as generous with money for his wife as he might have been. His main vice was chain smoking and wasting his money on his addiction, as well as ruining his health.

[12] While he was in the home he experienced being struck by golden arrows. He found it very profound but utterly mysterious.

from myself. Well, even that didn't wake me up, so I had to go through 'the dark night of the soul' and that was really dreadful. The golden arrows heralded the suffering but I am so grateful for them – they gave me a new dimension and terrible would have been my lot over here if I hadn't earned a bit of merit in my last few months. Of course, there are patches of my life which are light and music that has been my saviour – at least I was able to contribute something through that but my selfishness was my downfall and it's difficult to see the light for all the darkness I created for myself. I know I must overcome it but there are no short cuts.

Thanks for listening, Barb. I don't wish to be depressive but you, at least, understand a little of what I am going through. I have been seeing so much of my past life and it's taken over all my thoughts. Of course, you realise that I have to create a lot out of myself and my own imagination. I never knew much about flowers so will need some expert advice to help me plan a garden. I'll make it as colourful as I can and have some water and fountains and it will be sunny and peaceful. Your Mum will enjoy herself over here, I'm sure. If we get tired of anything we just recreate it in our minds.

I don't think I can write anymore now. I am going into slumber and I will receive some colour healing. I have got very low looking at my life and I need a boost of energy so that I can overcome the slow vibes. The old boy says it's better for me not to keep going home as it's upsetting. He says I can tune in with your thoughts without going into earth vibrations all the time, which make me feel heavy. I'm a new boy and have so much to learn. If only I hadn't been such a doubting Thomas.

Remember, none of us start on Earth with a clean sheet; we all bring many things with us from the past. I dread having to look at my other lives; the last one has been enough of a bombshell. However, I'm told in time I'll get stronger and there's no hurry to go back further. This is why we all need healing to strengthen us when we come here. It will be lovely when I've worked things through and can look ahead instead of back. Love to you all, especially your Mum.

Chapter Eight
More News

5th March 1987

Morning, Barb, That's a funny picture you have of me; couldn't you get a better one? I was a handsomer chap than that, you know! In fact, I think you'd like the way I look now. I'm slimmer and a good deal younger – quite fresh-faced. In fact, though I hate to admit it, I look younger now than you. Well, enough of that nonsense but you see I haven't lost my sense of humour and thank the Lord for that.

Since I last wrote, things have become calmer for me. I am able to see in more perspective and realise I'm not the worst chap who ever lived, even though I was shattered to see my wasted life pattern. It is heartrending how the arid parts take on all prominence. However, the old boy, who says I can call him 'Fred' – you see, he has a sense of humour too, has shown me some of the brighter aspects but the darker areas seemed to outnumber the bright. Nevertheless, he has helped me to see how I can overcome this. I shall be given the opportunity of re-birth when I am ready because the earth is in need of souls who can remember their soul pattern. I do hope that when I come again I will be able to retain more of that.

I wanted my own way too much and was frustrated and miserable because my ego wasn't satisfied. What a fool I was. The really important things are often what we push aside on earth.

'Fred' is a very knowledgeable chap but he doesn't give much away; he leaves me to work it out for myself. He says that's the only real way of learning.

I could talk a lot about each one of you. I've learned a bit more through seeing my own life. The patterns are tremendous. I don't only see as on a film with solid images but see patterns of colour; the life patterns and links. Would you believe it, we've all been together so often in the past, in countless lifetimes in different ways. The relationships and even the sex have changed around but still, the connections go on. I haven't yet seen separate lives in detail, only been shown through the graphs as it were. You've no idea how complex it is even with family ties, let alone friends and acquaintances. The Law[13] is exact; phew, it stunned me. Funny we don't remember anything because I had a life before this, so presumably, I saw the outcome of that when I 'died'. I wonder why we don't learn. I don't think I was such a bad chap last time either but obviously still had

---

[13] Of cause and effect

a heck of a lot to account for. I still have the earth vibes so strongly that I'm drawn back and would like to make a better shot of it next time. Your mum shouldn't be that long in coming [14] so I'll wait for her and see what she's going to do. It would be great if we could go in together. I still have a lot to make up to her but I seem to be developing courage and feel so much stronger than I did on earth. I was such a lily-livered chap and did all I could to buck trouble and responsibility. Now I must go; sorry I haven't got much of interest to relate yet. I'm mainly tuned into myself here except for 'Fred' who is supervising my struggles. Otherwise, I go home and look in on the others. I realise they are not likely to be able to converse with me but it's nice to know they think of me kindly and miss me as I do them. Give them all my love. I don't feel so bad when I go home now. The colour healing is lovely and gives me strength and optimism. Pity we're all such fools on earth and pay so little heed and attention[15]. Oh, well better luck next time. Bye, darling. Tune in again soon but don't overtire yourself. All my love, Dad.

7th March 1987
Hello again, Barb.

Thanks for tuning in. I was aware of all the lovely healing which went on in your room last night[16]. What truly lovely people you all are and what a delight it was to be in your presence. There was a Great Spirit in your midst; I don't know if it was actually the Christ but I would say that it was certainly one of his messengers. The radiance was outstanding and I felt all the better for it, like warming myself at a fire. There were others with me too. No one I knew but all derived benefit from being there. The colours were flashing and sparkling like jewels and I am sure you'll all be the better for it too.

My guide helps me but I was rather out of control at first, coming home through sheer force of emotion and not knowing how to handle the vibes. Now I realise if I can stay unemotional, I can handle things much better and have full control. I don't know how I would have managed without 'Fred'. He is a tower of strength, never letting go, however miserable I may have been. Saying little but calmly coaxing and urging me on. It must be awful for him having to watch others undergo the remorse they feel on seeing their 'playback'. I can't tell you how even the trivial little things rankle. I broke your mum's heart many a time and was unaware of the depth of the hurt. She did so want me to be loving and kind. Really, that was all she asked. She never craved riches or things for herself. It didn't matter whether I earned a fortune or not but my moods really did for her. Now I realise why she was so aggressive at times; it was a sort of safety valve and she had to harden her skin.

Anyway, you can imagine how lonely and lost I felt at first. I can't say it has all suddenly become sweetness and light because I'd be kidding myself but I'm beginning to realise what I have to do to repent. That word is very inadequate.

---

[14] She lived for another nine years
[15] To what comes afterwards
[16] With the meditation group

All the repentance in the world will not make a lot of difference to a life that's been lived – what is written is written but I am now seeing it clearly. I see the causes behind effects and find it difficult to pardon myself. The beauty of it is I'm being allowed to make up for it. I shall be learning all over again and I pray with all my might that I can retain my soul picture when I come again.

Do remember I'm not much different now from when I arrived here. I'm not omnipotent or clairvoyant because I've arrived here. I keep telling you what a new boy I am. Fortunately, I always had a love of beauty and of nature. You remember how I always loved to get you kids into the countryside. I loved the greenery and the open spaces and was never more at ease with myself than when I lived on the rifle range in Worcestershire towards the end of the war. Of course, I missed the family but it was as if I were two people – the town dweller with a family and the bachelor communing with nature – happy to spend time alone – to read and to listen to the Voice of Mother Nature. Next time around I'll try to live in a country environment to tend flowers and living things; yes, even grow herbs and learn their properties. My main concern now is to help others. It's a terrible thing to be selfish and I warn you, Barb, fight the tendency to want things your own way and never look down on the chance to serve and help others. It's a thousand times better than helping yourself which doesn't really lead anywhere.

My main stumbling block was the way I treated your mother and the reason I am so obsessed with her. She really came into the fray much more than any of you others. I don't have so much to make up for there, although there are things, of course, but the real reparation is to your mum, God bless her. I suppose I was jealous of her because she always seemed so capable. Her music came so easily to her and I never valued my singing as much as her playing. Mind you, I've learned now that that is nonsense. I was just as talented in my own way and should have worked at that and become more fully qualified. God gave me the gift of voice but I neglected it; I almost finished it off with smoking. I never realised how dedicated one must be and that the gift is only the first step and that one's purpose is to develop it so that when one returns to Spirit, one has more to show for it than when one left.

Do everything for the love of it, because in the end that's all there is, and the only thing that counts is to do everything with love. Giles is a wise soul[17] and is already getting a kick out of performing and giving people pleasure in return. I have to laugh at him although, of course, I really admire him, but it makes me smile to see the things he's already capable of. He puts himself down when he has no need but better that way, modesty is much better than having a big head.

Pop[18] was amongst those who came to greet me. There were so many I was flabbergasted. Some were people I hardly knew. Anyway, Pop brought his sisters too. They all rallied round and John was with Pop. They made a nice little group and although they meet up from time to time, they all live at different levels and have their own work and interests. Pop is very interested in new forms of

---

[17] My son then aged 16
[18] My father-in-law who died in 1981

transport which are due on the earth. He is way beyond me; in fact, he is much in advance of the others and I find it hard to hold his vibration because he's so advanced to my present stage. He understands me because he has been through my stage and said he was lonely and miserable at first. His mother helped him and was his constant companion when he visited earth. He was pleased to have John too. After a short time of review, he was able to move to a higher level and doesn't come into earth conditions as they are like a cold, clammy fog. However, he knows what is going on and is following Giles's career and keeping an eye on Chris's mum and Dorothy (her sister).

He is pleased with the way Reg[19] has coped on his own and said that he has a fine holding position on the island. (Jersey) He's built up something which will benefit you when you get there as the house is meant as a base for your work and relates to the ancient power there. I don't pretend to understand all this but I expect I will in time.

What a pity I spent so much of my latter years reading rubbish when there was so much of fascination I missed. I do wish I had spent more time speculating on what was to come and trying to learn more. I should be in a better way now. I need instruction from my guide and others who deal with groups of people such as me. I'm looking forward to making new acquaintances in my own position. I couldn't cope with those more advanced whose colours are lovely; my own are very shabby at present and this embarrasses me. I know they understand but even so, I don't feel like going amongst them until I can hold my own. Also, our minds are open books. Nothing can be hidden. It's like Cinderella not wanting to go to the ball because she was dressed in rags. Unfortunately, there's no fairy Godmother to provide rich finery – everything has to be provided by our own achievements; so you see, I have a way to go yet. Don't be worried about me, what I am going through is inevitable and we are all warned but we take no notice. The Bible tells us to live by the Law of Love but we don't listen. Just keep sending love and light, that's the best you can do. I'm being drawn away now. All my love, Dad.

10th March 1987
Dear Barb,

Hello again; phew, what a relief to get through once more. I know you're busy but it is lovely to have the chance to write when you can spare the time. I've been hanging around on the off chance. I know you've had a letter from your mum today; it breaks my heart when she's lonely and miserable. Tell her I'm always with her – in thought at least. I have to ask her to forgive me, really consciously forgive me – I have to know that she does because until she admits it with her whole heart, I cannot progress but will be held here by my own sense of unworthiness.

---

[19] His wife's brother

48

As I review my life, I see there are others to whom I must make reparation but they are as nothing compared to your mum. I love her more than life itself. Oh, why was I so dumb – if only I could have told her this and shown her; things would have been so different. We would have been a devoted couple. I didn't see it for myself – only in the last few months and when I came here it hit me like a bombshell. However, God is good; we do all get second chances and I want to take mine with your mum. There is so much to make up for.

With the better weather coming, she'll cheer up and I would like to see her get out a bit more. She's so good with people and gives them a lift. There are many who'd be glad of her company in her immediate area. You'd be amazed at how many lonely people there are. They put on a good face to outsiders but at home behind closed doors; they give way to their despair and feeling of uselessness. We can all do so much in small ways to show that we care. When people are retired, they have the time but not always the means to get about but even just popping into a neighbour's can do so much to promote cheerfulness.

At present, your mum needs building up herself but later she'll feel better and more able to join in. I hope she'll get round to playing again.[20] Tell her not to worry that she won't hear me sing; I'll be joining in every time, I can assure her of that.

Our Cis[21] has been to see me and George. They've settled down well here but are still very interested in what's going on at home, particularly with their grandson.[22] They say he has seen them and often talks to them when he's alone. Children are more aware than we give them credit for. Tim[23] is often led astray by entities he picks up – he's a very psychic child and needs to be watched. He must be shown the very best influences otherwise he'll make contact with the less desirable. Sue[24] is very psychic too. The trouble is that people don't realise they're vulnerable and they need to know how to protect themselves. It is only too easy to open up. I realise I did that too and often my tempers and disagreeableness were brought on by outside aspects. This is not to excuse myself but to show you these elements are always around and ready to pounce when they spot an opening.

You are right to tell people to link with the Forces of Light, Barb, this is wonderful protection but it's no good people saying that and doing the opposite. There has to be integrity all along the way or one is done for.

I don't want to depress anybody merely to state the facts as I see them from my present standpoint. As I said, I haven't gone far yet, so I see the conditions very close to the earth. I suppose there is light further on and goodness but I wouldn't know much about that yet. I have caught a glimpse of some lovely places but have also been tuned into less lovely ones. You see, we don't realise but so much is in our own mind, of our own making. We are the creators. I think

---

[20] She was a pianist
[21] His eldest sister and her husband
[22] Scott, who was then a little boy
[23] Albert's youngest grandson
[24] Tim's mother, Albert's youngest daughter

this is what is meant when they say we're made in God's image. God creates everything – He's created us and we also create things and conditions. On earth, it is not so apparent because we can't see thoughts and what they create but here the mind world is everything. I know that when I can forgive myself and like myself more, I shall have a grand chance of living in a healthier atmosphere and better place. When I am more at peace with myself, I shall expand and that way, I'll be able to create things and places of beauty. Hopefully, by the time your mum reaches me I'll be in a better case and will have a lovely place for her to come to then we'll decide together what we want to do. Once she releases me by truly forgiving me I shall start to live again.

I asked him
Q: Have you seen your mother yet?
A: Not that I'm aware of consciously but I believe she has been to me in my healing sessions. I awake with the most beautiful and blessed sense of being cosseted, like a child being tucked in by a mother at bedtime.
Q: Have you seen your dad?

A: He was amongst those who came to meet me but I don't feel we shall have a lot to do with each other because we did not have sufficient affinity on earth. He didn't care deeply enough for me or I for him. He came as a duty because I was his son and although very kind and concerned, there isn't a deep enough bond to hold us closely together – we are more like acquaintances. I did love my mother's sister, Amy. She was kind to us as children and I have visited her. She is a busy woman caring for the less fortunate coming over from earth.

Once I have sorted myself out I want to 'freelance' for a while to see the sort of places and people there are and to see what sort of work I'd be attracted to. Mind you, whatever I decide to do I shall have to receive training. 'Fred' says when I'm ready he'll pass me on to those in charge. I have to decide though; it won't be decided for me. What we do over here we have to do with our whole hearts when we decide to give service.

Of course, many at this lower level just suit themselves for years. You have to have developed a conscience and can see your mistakes; then give yourself gladly in service, in however humble a capacity.

Q: You said you would like to help with scientific discoveries.

A: Yes, in theory, I would but it's like saying you'd like to be a brain surgeon. It's pie in the sky unless you get trained and first of all, you have to have the capacity.

Well, Barb, I've given you a few things to think about and must let you go. Give my love to the others and best of all to your darling mum. Tell her she's always in my thoughts. I'm like a love-sick swain these days. She's feeling depressed because as I draw into her aura she's sensitive enough to pick up my vibrations and as I am so aware of my short-comings I automatically bring my heaviness with me. Tell her I'm trying to overcome that and to bring more cheerfulness. With all my love, Dad.

PS: I'd like you to have a better photo of me so you can show your pupils.

Chapter Nine
Improvement

15th March 1987

Dear Barb, What an absolute delight to write again. Thanks so much.[25] My train of thought was broken but I appreciate you all have things to do and it's not always convenient to stop and tune in. Pity though because things were going smoothly.

Well, I'm sure you'll be glad to know I'm feeling much better. 'Fred' is very pleased with my progress. For the first time I'm starting to feel at home and to look around to see the possibilities. It has made such a difference to me to see that I'm accepted, that you all know I have simply gone away but am not dead and can still be in touch. I feel extraordinarily privileged and think about how many people would like to be in the same boat as me. It really is great. I know your mum is feeling better too and when I go home I can take my cheerier outlook with me. Really, it's a good feeling to know that despite your worst faults, you're still accepted and loved for yourself. It's so good that the others are coming around to accept the reality of these letters. Give them time; it's a lot to swallow all at once. I would have been the first to be sceptical as you know. But there, we live and learn! Funny that you have to be 'dead' to really know what it is to live! Anyway, it gladdens my heart that our Edna[26] is so fascinated by it all. God bless her for her open mind. I really admire her for that because as I've said I could never have accepted so readily.

Harry[27] has been here too. He's been trying for years to contact Edna and has been all round the family trying to find an opening. (*He did once get through to me (Barbara) but wasn't able to hold the vibrations for long enough to deliver a message*). He now feels there's more possibility of contacting Edna through this writing. Harry wants you to tell Edna that he was devastated when he realised he'd gone over[28] and left her with so much to handle.[29] He was desperate to communicate with her to tell her what to do but apart from meeting your mum and Jenny[30] in dreams and Edna's awareness of his presence, he couldn't get any

---

[25] We were disturbed by my son using the telephone.

[26] His youngest sister, who lived to be 103.

[27] Edna's late husband

[28] He died instantly of a heart attack as they were about to go shopping.

[29] Regarding his business

[30] Harry's daughter

sense through. He was glad of the prayers sent out for him as they helped to calm him and gradually he settled down. He and his mum became really good friends and he found her so helpful. They never really saw eye-to-eye on earth and there were often frictions but she's done all she can to make up for that and really showed him the ropes. His dad has gone on further but often returns to see them. Harry still retains his interest in making things work and is always busy creating new-fangled things or learning how things tick.[31]

They're all delighted about the new baby[32] and will keep a watch over her. They say not to worry about the eyes – the condition will soon clear up. This frequently happens because after the darkness of the womb the light can be too strong for the delicate eyes, especially from artificial light and the fluorescent tubes found in hospitals. Keep them clean and bathed in soft, warm water with cotton wool and the condition will improve. Try to keep her away from direct light and in daylight as much as possible. At night, small lamps are better than a main light.

Through Albert, Harry told Edna that life would become better for her and her worries would be overcome. He said he couldn't bear to see her lonely and miserable. Hers was a cheerful, sunny disposition and she put on a brave face to others. However, he wanted her to get out and about more as she could be missing out on something great by staying at home. He was delighted that they now had a 'telepathic telephone' but said, "It's jolly difficult from both sides to get a message over but Son[33] says she (Barbara) is getting good at holding his vibes and this makes it easier for others to write with her too. She'll gradually get it to a fine art. Often she doesn't trust herself and lets her mind block the creative process but she's doing alright. It's only natural to doubt and wonder how much comes from her mind and how much from others. There's bound to be a mixture – if we didn't have her mind to work through we couldn't make contact."

Harry: "Anyway, Ed, I think you're great and I look forward to be able to send more 'letters' to you. If there's anything you want to ask me just send out a thought. Don't expect me to know everything. I may know a bit more than you but just dying doesn't give you the key to the universe; we still have to make it step by step. Son wants to finish off now so I'll say cheerio and send you and the family all my sincerest love. Your Harry."

Well, Barb, you see, you've made somebody else very happy. It's worth the time you've given to it. Now you can get on with your music. Keep calm and

---

[31] When I first got my computer, I often needed help. One day, knowing how keen Harry had always been on gadgets, I called on him to sort me out. Suddenly, the whole thing went completely haywire and when my IT man came to rescue me, he couldn't make out what had happened but said he had never seen anything like it before. I didn't tell him I had asked a 'dead' man to help me nor did I call on Harry again.

[32] Harry's granddaughter, Lianne

[33] The family name for her brother, Albert

just give it all you've got; you can't go wrong. Love to your mum and all the others, your much happier Dad.

17th March 1987

Dear Barb, I've been to attend a ceremony. It was lovely, so light and such a power of lovely singing. We all stood in groups. Each group wore a different colour and we all sang. It was a paean of praise to the Almighty, to the Great Powers of Life on all levels, in all forms. You've no idea of the feeling of expansion of peace, love and joy. It was worth all I've been through to experience that. I wore a sort of yellow colour – more of an ochre colour really. I'm not sure what it signifies but I am now to start my training. This was an initiation ceremony where we are sorted out and put into grades. I am with a group of six people, two women and four men. We are to form a cell as it were and will learn together in this small group. From time to time we will meet with the larger group. This is a power ceremony to build our auras and to instil optimism and cheer into us, to enable us to progress. I am so grateful to 'Fred' who can now take a breather himself because he sees I am more capable of standing on my own feet, thanks to the family and those who care about me in Spirit. It is really lovely when you begin to realise the immensity and loveliness of this realm.

I am now beyond the grey area that I seemed to inhabit for so long – there was nothing there, just a grey mist and I was only aware of 'Fred' most of the time because I was so locked away in myself. Now, I am aware of others and of the concern of many who care for me and who were so sorry to see me in a bad way, lonely and miserable and so homesick. That is now passing, I am aware of a beautiful mellow light in which everything is bathed. It is quite beautiful, warming and comfortable. I now see there are lots of people around me if I wish to let them in. I was so sad at first because my colours were awful, yet now I realise pride is useless, people accept you as you are, not as on earth where they look down on you if you're shabby. Consequently, as I feel better about myself, my colours are shining out and I feel I can hold my own. I have a way to go but at least I can now face people and talking to those in my group I realise I am not alone in my attitude; they have only been here a relatively short time and felt just as I did, shattered at the way they'd lived their lives.

I am now aware of other guides besides 'Fred', the guides of those others. 'Fred' now has companions of his own ilk and as he doesn't have to watch my every move, he can relax more. It was good to see Harry; he's such a down to earth sort of chap – no histrionics, like me. It couldn't have been easy for him at first but he's made it and so will I. He's so balanced and level headed with regard to Edna and delighted that she will see his letter and know how he feels about her. She's a good sister to me too and I really love her, as I do your mum and all of you. What a lucky chap I am to have such a family; I'm so proud of you all and will do all I can to help you.

14th April 1987

Oh, what a relief to tune in again and know I'm not forgotten. It's seemed a long time since I made contact. I know you've been busy and I do appreciate you have other things to do and others to look after. You really spread yourself very well, Barb. I think you're doing a grand job. You don't get much time to yourself these days and you do need to recharge your own batteries.

Your mum is going to the Spiritualist Church and I feel very sad that she seems to prefer Ernie[34] to me. I can't grumble though, she was a good wife. I hope it will sort itself out and that she'll want to be with me when she comes over. Of course, I see things differently now and know I can't be selfish but must share. It has been a shattering and salutary experience and was totally unexpected. I didn't realise just what self-judgement we would experience. It is the trivial things, well, seemingly small things, which rankle. I never considered myself a wicked chap though I know I was far from perfect and could not live up to my own would be standards but to feel as I do over things I was unaware about at the time; well, you know, Barb, or at least you have some idea of how it's been. Yes, it is improving to some extent but I think it will be a while before I'm out of the darkness. I long for the light; keep shining it on me but at present, I cannot take too much radiance; it's too strong for me. I long for peace of mind and know I over chastise myself but don't seem able to help it. I need your healing just as much as any physical patients. Truly, I do. It was comforting to be able to get through to the medium at your mum's church but rather frustrating. I would so like to talk to her face to face.

I don't know why I can't seem to meet her in her sleep state. I have tried but it's difficult and I always just seem to miss her, perhaps if she really and truly wanted to be with me we could meet but although she misses me to some extent; it is rather through habit than desire, and this is a hurt I have to live with. I think I cared for her more than she did for me but I neglected to let her know how much and our personalities did clash, as you know. She often irritated me and yet I cared for her very deeply; nevertheless. I must develop patience and hope that in time things will improve but I now have to face the fact that she may desire to be with others or elsewhere when she finally makes the transition.

I feel rather sad and lonely and know I have to fend for myself. How headstrong we are when we're young and how eternal life seems. None of us think we're going to die. We see it happen to others but think we're eternal. I know there are other places to move on to because I've had glimpses, but I seem to be holding myself back. Once I can get release from my own frustrations and disappointments and like myself more, things will improve. I'm glad of your prayers, they make me feel warm and comfortable, please continue.

Yes, others have tried to help me but I'm not very good company yet. I feel so lost and helpless and need a good deal of healing. I do get looked after from time to time. I am taken to a lovely place where there is light and colour and other patients; then I sleep and dream and experience another reality.

---

[34] He was her boyfriend before she met Albert.

I had the opportunity to join a group and to commence a period of learning but I can't concentrate yet; I am not able to get free of myself to expand into group work. I am still absorbed with my own shortcomings. 'Fred' is not with me so often but I do see him from time to time. He cares for me, I know and is unhappy to see me thus. I long for love and light and for my dear ones around me.

I am aware of Michaela's[35] plight but don't seem to have any influence over her. She has to make her own way, as we all do. Send her all the love and light you can and any material help; it will be good for your own development but will also help to raise her morale. It's never easy when you leave home and go to another town, especially with work to find. I took the easy way out too often and failed to grow. She must be encouraged to stand on her own feet. None of us can ride on somebody else's bandwagon.

I will do the best I can to impress thoughts and co-incidences are a good way of waking people up. I do so long to be of use and know I must do all I can to be ready for the work which is waiting. I haven't done anything about a home yet. I don't need one at present as I float about a lot. I like the countryside and try to envisage where I would like to be but I don't think you fully realise how deep into myself I am. I cannot overcome my thoughts and I miss you all so much. I am trying but it's far from easy. Nothing is given to us on a plate – all has to be earned. If we learned that in life we'd all be better for it. We cannot expect anything from anybody.

Of course, I'm not the only one in this boat, there are many in a worse case, but it doesn't make it any better. The others here all have their own lives to lead and I don't want to be a burden. I prefer to sort myself out alone for the time being. God bless you, Barb, I'm off now. Take care of yourselves and know that your dad loves you dearly. I am going to sink into sleep.

Due to Barbara's many commitments and probably the fact that Albert was growing stronger, there was a gap in the letter from April to November.

8th November 1987

Hello there, dear Barb, Lovely to make contact again. I'm sorry to hear about your friend Cyril[36] – what a nice chap he is. I really appreciated his singing when I heard him in Redditch – just the sort of tenor I like – pure, not heavy and with a lovely sense of line and an immaculate delivery and phrasing. These things often happen to the nicest people. He will not lose out by it, however, but will derive strength from such suffering and will know what it is to have friends praying for him and of the love of his family. We all have to make the journey – there's no gainsaying that and to be at peace and ready for it, as he is, is a blessing and a boon when you think how many live in fear and dread as I did.

---

[35] His granddaughter
[36] The tenor Cyril Somers with whom Chris and I often sang, who had been diagnosed with terminal cancer of the spine

Well, there's nothing to it and I'm here to prove it. He has been given time to prepare which is a blessing you know. It's a terrible wrench and shock for those who die suddenly in accidents. It takes a while for them to become acclimatised, believe me. Just keep praying for him, that's all you can do and it's never wasted.

Now do give Chris my best for his performances and tell him he'll have quite a line-up there, including yours truly and Ralph[37]. Of course, Harold[38] will be there and John – that's what they wanted you to know when they contacted you yesterday. Anyhow, there'll be quite a queue for seats. Lucky we don't need tickets, isn't it? And the fact that space is no object to us. As many as want to will be able to see it and many of us link over here, due to our love and consideration for you all and of all you are doing to promote health and wellbeing and to bring light to those who search.

Well, tell Chris his grandparents – all four of them, will be in the front row and so many friends and relatives, including Keith Erwen, (*a fellow student and colleague*) who has become quite a chum of mine. He's got a great sense of humour and is now overcoming the state in which he came over. He too is grateful for the prayers and wants you to know he won't forget you.

We all want to support Chris – he deserves it and all his hard work won't go unnoticed. Just keep your peckers up and keep as you are and you won't go wrong.

---

[37] My cousin who died a few months after Dad.
[38] Chris's father and uncle.

Chapter Ten

Reconnection

1st December 1987

I did not hear from Dad for almost a month then he came through once more.

Are you ready? Start the pen, that way I can get contact. Glad to be with you again. Your mother pleases me by doing her best to keep optimistic. Yes, she is a worrier by nature and needs to overcome that but she's trying, bless her. Ralph has come over a little short of his time. He is ecstatic though, at how well he is and just can't believe how different he feels in such a short time.[39] He was met by his mum and dad, his Aunt Rose, Uncle Ernie and sundry friends and acquaintances. He is alright; don't worry about him. He is well and truly on the way to Heaven. He gave support and joy to many people and did all he could to see that others were alright. He was good and upright in his dealings and will now learn to let himself go in ways which he would not have found possible on earth. He is going to be kept busy.[40]

As he was short of his time,[41] he will be working very close to the earth plane. He is interested in healing and hopes that he will be able to help earth doctors to halt and arrest the disease[42] which killed him.

It would have been better if Ralph could have stayed longer in the body but he continued to grow weaker, so it was decided that as he had a healthy astral counterpart, his physical body should be relinquished. He would like to communicate with Sheila[43] but was never easily at home expressing himself in writing so I will act as proxy. You know how easy I have always found writing because I could say in print what I could never express with the spoken word and communicating with you in this way is great. I feel I could go on forever and will till the power is used up. Thank your crystals; they are supplying more energy than you know.

There is a vast amount of energy stored in the earth. It would take your scientists by surprise if they realised one-tenth. They get themselves in a state over coal, gas and nuclear energy but the very rocks they stand on are bursting

---

[39] He died of lung cancer at the age of 68

[40] During one of my meditation sessions, I found myself going down a dark tunnel but came out into a beautiful landscape bathed in golden light. A kind of village fete was taking place with lots of people, including Ralph who was thoroughly enjoying himself.

[41] On Earth.

[42] Cancer

[43] Ralph's wife

with energy waiting to be unleashed. But enough of that, this is meant to be about Ralph's progress. We digest light and colour as you do food; however, although we don't need food, when they first come over, some folk want the sort of things they've known and enjoyed on earth. Nobody bothers them and if that's what they like, that's what they have so long as they fancy it but later they grow out of that and realise that the astral body only uses light – it is all it needs to fuel and drive it. That is why it is so malleable. We move at the speed of thought (faster than the speed of light on earth) and within our own limits (due to our own stage of development) are able to be in several areas at once. As I told you before, we live in a mind universe far more than you do. Our bodies react immediately to our least thought. It is quite bewildering at first and a bit like being in a dream where everything is illogical and lacking sequence. The more you can train your minds on Earth to be one pointed, the more helpful it will be when you come over here. [44]

That is not to say be rigid or narrow; far from it, but this is why you are told to concentrate on one thing at a time and give your full attention to it and learn and assess things in the light of reality.[45] The main thing for Sheila to know is that Ralph is truly alive and kicking and will not desert her. She can live with him in her head[46] if she wishes and there will be a true blending of minds. Gradually, she will not miss the physical link so much because she will realise that she has gained in proportion to what she has lost.

Start taking iron, Barbara; living in the inner world is essential but has to be in balance with the outer world. Do not limit yourself in any way; just keep your equilibrium. You have not been given the path of the mystic. You are a communicator – your place is out in the world. You are doing good work even when you don't think you are doing anything. There are so many levels of doing and being. Bless you, for all the sensitivity and diligence you apply to everything but don't forget to take time off for fun – realise the tonic effect of laughter and the ability to switch off is very necessary to recharge the batteries and give strength to the next phase.

All love to you, my darling. I don't want to sign off but fear I must in case I run the risk of overcharging your batteries. We are dealing with real energies and I don't want to overtax your system. Keep sending your prayers to me – they enable me to achieve more than I could simply in my own light – they build my energies and tune my colours beautifully. I am now holding my own in the aural spectrum stakes, you'll be glad to know, and it's all thanks to you and your girls.[47]

---

[44] It is interesting that lots of people on Earth are now beginning to practice 'mindfulness'.

[45] The practice of 'mindfulness' is becoming popular among many people in the second decade of the twenty-first century.

[46] Telepathically.

[47] Members of the meditation group

Ralph thanks you for the prayers and all you've done, and asks you to continue with them and for Sheila and Tim[48]. We're just a great cosmic family – ain't it grand?!

20th December 1987

Thanks, Barb, I've been watching over your shoulder and am interested at what I wrote through you and how things have changed for me. I thought you'd like to know and be brought up to date.

Well, 'Fred' as we call him, has been able to take time off for a while now and just looks in from time to time to assure himself all is well; or if I need him, he comes to me in thought. He is a soul from a higher level of life whose work and duty it is to care for those of a lower order. I am truly grateful to him and now understand what he was trying to convey to me.

I have been able to forgive myself more than I thought I would. Of course, it doesn't make up for my misdeeds or omissions but it does get things into perspective and enables me to see the difficulties and tribulations of the human condition in a clearer light. It doesn't matter that we have to try and try again – in each lifetime we discover and experience different aspects and this brings such richness to the soul. Even suffering has its place and if we cannot learn any other way, we develop through our sufferings. Life cannot be fully experienced just at a physical level. There are too many unseen elements. It is only as we progress through successive lives that real living becomes apparent and we begin to see the essence which lies behind the apparently material element. What is written is written – there is no way I can alter past mistakes – they are there for all time, as on a tape recording, but I shall progress through those very things that at first seemed so devastating.

Death, although an illusion, is very necessary because it is only on the next layer as it were, that everything becomes clearer. It is assessment time and when we can forgive ourselves, we can forgive others. Our understanding grows, so we would never presume to judge the other chap. It is only ignorance that causes us to judge.

Who knows, one day, even I may do the kind of work that 'Fred' does. Already in a small way, I help souls who are a bit disorientated when they get here. I have some good friends, better than I would have thought, people who quite took to me on earth and who appreciated my friendship, or would, if I'd given them the chance but I was always basically a solitary soul, though I could be humorous and lively among company. I was staggered at all the people who'd enjoyed and gained from my singing. That was a real bonus to me but I should have been more aware and applied myself to music with more dedication. However, I'm now making up for lost time and my voice is fresh and green and I'm learning all over again. Tell your mum I'm also learning the piano – yes, odd as it may seem, that is possible – I have a piano of etheric substance. The important thing is my desire to do so. It was something I always wanted on earth

---

[48] Their adopted son

and was the reason I was jealous of your mother's gift. I never admitted it but I'd have loved to play. As she was already good at it, I couldn't face having to start from scratch so I let it put me off. I thought I couldn't afford lessons but we can always find cash for the things we really want and a few cigarettes a week would have paid for it. Imagine your mum's face if I'd tried to outdo her playing!

Well, that's all in the past. Music over here is a lovely thing, healing and creative. Yes, there is the destructive side to sound, of course, but there is no destruction in real terms, only a change of vibration.

As music was one of the things I loved most, I am making it my work. For a while, Billy[49] and I did a bit of sight-seeing together[50]. We'd always got on well and had the same background but he'd acquired a bit more culture than me. Anyway, we trotted around the world together seeing places we'd never had a chance to visit and quite enjoyed ourselves. However, it was a mixed blessing because there are some sad places on earth. We did what we could, where we could and you know me, how I've always loved kiddies; well, if I came across an unhappy child I did my best to leave some feeling of love and warmth in its aura. Many a time I've been saddened to see the poor, hungry little mites and have called on those capable of helping them, both on our side and to impress the thoughts of those in the flesh.

To come back to my level: I now have a little house which is very light and bright but I live alone because I need rest and recuperation. However, I visit lots of friends and they, me and because of the music I've been drawn into areas of like-minded souls, some who were known on earth, others not. At my level, there are still many desires to fulfil and there are disappointments to be worked through. However, it's much easier here 'cos we don't have to earn a living.

I have much to thank my mother for; she sang to me when I was a child and she had a lovely voice that awakened in me a love of the human voice which has never left me. My mother's essence reaches me and enfolds me like a warm liquid but she is now impersonal in her current aspect. However, for certain tasks, she can assume her old personality but does not do so normally, only for important occasions, like coming through a medium (Christine Holohan in 1982) to let you know that she was interested in you. Your singing drew her to you and she appreciates the love you pour into your music. Never think it's wasted. You will discover a world of music awaiting you here, which you have created for yourself and which will take you by surprise.

I am very settled now – I can tune in with the family when I want to and can see what they are experiencing in a new and unemotional way. At present, I am working to learn more about music and its potent qualities and later I will work with it in a direct way in the realm of creativity.

I just wanted you to know how I have come home on this side and how much more adjusted I am in every way. Can't you tell from my thoughts which I am

---

[49] A friend from his childhood who had worked at the Birmingham Art Gallery and Museum

[50] Seeing the astral counterpart of the earth.

impressing on yours, just how much happier and vital I am? You know from the degree of light permeating my environment that I am in good fettle, don't you?

Be optimistic, be bright because however bad or grey things may seem, the sun is always shining somewhere and the soul has its own home where all is well. Be grateful for your everyday life, even when it seems too mundane because it teaches you so much, and that will be yours for all time – making you grow and evolve until such time as you can transcend all the earthly planes and rise up to a new level of eternal development.

I still have much to learn and experience at this level but I know now that in time I shall pass out of this sphere and into a greater, even wider area of expansion but we shall never fail to be in contact because our web of love will link us forevermore.

19th January 1988
Dad's next letter dealt with a family crisis, giving advice which, unfortunately, was not taken by the individuals concerned. This failure led to tragedy some years later involving the first, then the second of his granddaughters.

It's no use any of you getting in a state about this; what is done is done and it's got to take its course. 'Fred' says it's all to the good for them if they win through. He doesn't often commit himself but I consulted with him and he seemed to think their better selves would overcome the self-centredness. (*They did not*).

Well, it's put your mum about and no mistake, wouldn't you know? Of course, she has always had to have something to worry about and this is a whopper. Sue is distraught at the thought of history repeating itself. She has so much to resolve within herself so she cannot take on board someone else's troubles. She is in a transitional stage herself and there's a lot of water to pass under the bridge.

Anyway, just encourage and uplift them all – you know the song and dance they make of everything. Just be kindly and loving and leave the rest to providence and innate goodwill. We all know that life is full of brickbats – but you now understand so much of the causes behind effects, so you can be more at peace within yourself. So be it then; till next time. Thanks for tuning in and still including me in family problems. All love, Dad.

Chapter Eleven
Healers and Teachers

With the advent of Maria and my connection with the College of Psychic Studies, we began meeting people with similar interests, particularly with regard to healing.

When Chris was singing with the Netherlands Opera, he became friendly with a baritone who was interested in healing, and when they returned to England, we invited him and his girlfriend, along with Christine, to our house. Of course, the talk soon turned to spiritual matters but I was surprised when Christine handed me the locket she was wearing and asked me to psychometrise it for her. I laughed as I had never tried such a thing before and was quite sure that I wouldn't be any good at it. However, she insisted, so I closed my eyes, placed it on my forehead and sat quietly; waiting for something to happen even though I suspected that it would be a waste of time.

To my surprise, I began to see pictures in my mind's eye, just like a moving film. There was a ruined church and children were climbing over the rubble. It was not a place I recognised but Christine encouraged me to report what I saw. I described the images but kept saying it was all tosh and I wanted to give the chain back to her. She said I had to go on because she recognised what I was seeing. After a while, the picture faded so I gave her back her chain. She totally accepted everything I saw and said that it was a church in Ireland that had been blown up in the 1920s. It was near her home and she and her friends often played there as children. I was amazed that I had seen everything so clearly and later asked friends to hand me items of jewellery so that I could practice.

The baritone's girlfriend then asked for healing because she had a painful back. We all closed our eyes and concentrated; suddenly, through my closed eyes, I was aware of a life size Native American Indian in the middle of the room. He wore a white buckskin suit with a large feather war bonnet with feathers reaching the floor, and grinned at me because he was aware that I could see him. Behind him was the figure of a young American Indian woman.

When the healing was over, I told Christine what I had seen, thinking that this time my imagination had really gone over the top. However, she said that it was White Feather, the teaching and healing guide who worked through her. He has a great sense of humour and is a truly wonderful being. Since then I have become aware that he is a teacher with many students and I have called on him from time to time for healing. I have learned a lot from him and of the Native American attitude to the earth. However, healing can take many forms, even with regard to inanimate objects. For instance, he is good with cars! My pianist Jillian bought a new car but it kept stalling in traffic. The garage mechanics couldn't solve the problem so advised returning it to the factory.

I called on White Feather. I don't drive and have no knowledge of engines but I saw a mental picture of the engine and was directed to a little shutter. I told Jill and she asked the garage if there was anything wrong in that area. There was; the shutter was open when it should have been closed. It was a small thing so had been overlooked and the car had probably come out of the factory like that. The mechanic adjusted it and there was no further trouble.

A few years later, we were staying in Cromer on a busy Saturday afternoon. By this time, Jill had another car but on this occasion, it refused to start. I mentally called on White Feather and shortly afterwards the engine sprang to life and off we went.

A similar incident happened in Jersey two years ago when my friend Teresa, who had bought a second-hand car, wanted to give it an airing so took me, Christine and her sister Mary, who was staying with us, out for a spin to Greve de Lecq on the north coast of the island. It was early evening and the restaurant and gift shop had closed so Teresa's car was the only one left in the car park. There wasn't a soul around and we were dumbfounded when the car refused to start. Again, I mentally called on White Feather, and suddenly, over a grassy knoll appeared the head, then the body of a young man, followed by a couple of friends. He was Polish and spoke little English but without any ado, came over to the car, opened the bonnet, fiddled with something, signalled to Teresa to start the ignition and all was well. The men disappeared as quickly as they had arrived and I suspect that White Feather had a hand in them being at the right place at the right time. Teresa drove us to our house then carried on across the island to her home without any further trouble.

Like many people, we have learned to ask for a parking place prior to a journey and nine times out of ten it works.

It is said that angels can take on human forms at certain times and I think this happened to me one stormy night when I lived in Harrow. I was on my way to teach at the adult education college in Stanmore and buses on that route were not frequent. I had to cross a busy feeder road to the MI and I was late. I knew that a bus was due but could not get across the road. It was dark and rain was lashing down so I was feeling desperate when suddenly a man appeared in the middle of the road and stopped the traffic. I could see the bus coming but he allowed me just enough time to sprint across and catch it. I turned to wave my thanks but he had completely disappeared. Quite uncanny!

For the first three years after Maria made contact through Christine, I became very aware of her and she knew what was going on in my life. She even told Christine that she thought Chris was funny the way he gargled as he cleaned his teeth! I had never thought about it before but I had to admit that he did make a funny sound. There was valuable advice on singing, with particular reference to roles on which I was working. One day, in 1983, Christine said Maria was showing her a Butterfly and we assumed that this was symbolic of transformation but it was more mundane than that because shortly afterwards, I received a phone call inviting me to sing in a production of 'Madame Butterfly' at a wonderful neo-baroque theatre in Lille in northern France. After I returned, I continued to see Christine and Maria often joined us. Now that I am more experienced in esoteric matters, I realise that we sometimes misinterpreted the information she gave us. Some of the events occurred over the next three decades and involved my son, who was destined to become a professional singer, though we did not know it at the time as he was still a schoolboy. In particular, Maria spoke of singing in Russia, being on BBC radio and of a production at the Royal Opera House, a TV series and a production of the 'Mikado' in America. A long time afterwards, we realised that this was all totally factual but the information was for Giles, not me. She also said that my sister's current relationship would never come to anything; this naturally upset her, but Maria was right and my sister could have been spared a lot of angst if she had put an end to it before it took too great a toll.

We also misread information about Mary going to America. At that time, her son who is the same age as my son was a schoolboy but later became a musician and it was he who went to America, not her.

Gradually, one learns to simply report the information and wait for time to deliver the event because it is easy for wishful thinking to get in the way.

During one of my meditation sessions, Maria told me that she was moving on. Much later, I discovered that she was now with Helena Hawley, who, although she was not a singer, was being trained in sound healing. Maria's work with me had run its course, though sometimes I feel her influence even though I finally retired from singing in 2012.

25th February 1988
Maria wrote:

I didn't come only to help you but also to help myself. I must admit, I needed to find someone I could help. There are many connections between us and I was delighted to find you and to work with you. How our work is now paying off. Are you not surprised at all the things you have tackled and accomplished on so many fronts? As I have been so closely associated with you, I have been able to contribute but also to learn, and what you have achieved has been my achievement too. We have learned together and I have effected many things for you and given you the ideas which you have accepted and followed.

Your classes have been very successful, though you are not fully aware of just how much has spun off in all sorts of areas. These ideas are now in the air and becoming more accepted. This is thanks to people such as you, who have assisted the Zeit Geist to bring about a new dispensation.

We have indeed worked hard with you, harder than you are aware – often when your conscious mind was elsewhere. Now, all the diverse strands will pull together. It is always difficult when you cannot see ahead and have to take so much on trust.

The time is coming when you will need to put it all in motion. Sleep well, keep strong – do not mollie-coddle yourself but do not overdo it. That is all I can say: believe me, I wish I could tell you more but it is not possible. Just know that I love and care for you as a sister, Your loving Maria. [51]

Maria didn't willfully withhold information from me; it was simply that so much would be asked of me during the next quarter-century, that I would have been so overwhelmed, I would never have got going. Everything I had ever learned was drawn upon. At school, I had taken business studies; on leaving school, I studied at the Birmingham College of Art. On leaving college, I worked for a short time in the Wardrobe Department of the Alexandra Theatre in Birmingham, but having seen my first opera, 'The Marriage of Figaro' my fate was sealed. I began to study singing with Mary Parsons and started to win prizes at competitive music festivals. I also took singing, theory and piano exams of the Associated Board of the Royal Schools of Music. Singing was now the be all and end all of my life but my salary at the theatre was risible, so as my new way of life required more income, I took a job as secretary to the radiographer in the X–Ray department at the Birmingham Dental Hospital. After two years I went into the commercial world, but finally ended up on the News staff of ATV, The Midlands.

In 1961, I won a major singing award, and then I applied for a place at the Guildhall School of Music and Drama in London, and was accepted. Here I met my husband, baritone, Christopher Davies, and we married eighteen months later. I sang many leading roles while still at Guildhall and on graduation, made my debut with the Arts Council's Opera for All company, singing major roles in three operas on extensive tours. The rest is history.

15th March 1988
Communication from my father.

Hello, Barb, lovely to contact you again. I'm never far away; often look in to see how you're getting on and I'm so glad all is going well. Chris uses up a lot of nervous energy which is why he doesn't put on weight but he's fine in himself. I see a nice healthy aura, full of colour and light. If everybody was like him the world would be a better place. Always remember to have enough rest, Barb, don't overcharge yourself.

Well, I wanted to talk to you about Mary; you rather over-stretched yourself in the advice you gave her. So much has to be taken on trust. That is the whole crux of the matter. If too much is given or expected, there is no chance of a lesson being thoroughly learned. It's alright, no harm done, but a little at a time. In essence, you spoke true. Now, I'm going to give you a chance to catch your breath; just wanted you to know I'm around and taking an interest. All love to you all, Dad.

---

[51] During a weekend workshop with Marie Louise Lacey, we were asked to pick an Angel card and mine was synthesis. I didn't know the meaning of the word but Chris, who is an educated chap, told me that it means a blending together of many different facets.

PS: I think you'll have to take these 'letters' away from your publisher friend – too slow, not enough action. Do get a move on. If you'd kept them in your own hands and taken them to the College of Psychic Studies in London, time would have been saved. Never mind, there will be more to come.

Ever since he first started writing his 'post mortem letters', he had wanted them published but the friend who offered to deal with them was a retired publisher who was worried about their effect on his orthodox friends, many of whom were retired clergymen. When he died, I let them hang fire because I didn't know anything about publishing. It was eight months before I heard from my father again.

Chapter Twelve
A Helping Hand

27th September 1988

Hello, Barb, Fancy you forgetting your old Dad. Well, not so old now; really feeling very youthful and bright. I've been with you in the typing of my old letters. Gosh, what a cry baby I was. It brought back all the old feelings of despair and despondency but yet it's been worth it if these 'letters' are published.

The book is to be more comprehensive than the letters of a 'new boy' in the spirit world but they are necessary because what I experienced is felt by so many. There's a big difference between now and then and less than a couple of years covered by your time. I was always a quick learner when I put my mind to anything and I was determined to get out of the 'hell hole' where I first found myself. Of course, the 'hell hole' was my own mind and my sense of disappointment and frustration put me in that area. Well, I've wiped all that from my feet now. I am newly born – fresh as a daisy. I have moved on and I live in a world of mellow light – golden and warm. Of course, there are areas of vast proportion way beyond where I am – brilliant in their expanded light; but I could not hold those frequencies yet. However, I am in better fettle and well pleased with my present abode.

Music has been my salvation. I could never have dreamed of the advances I have made. My will and desire to do so, of course, was the motive power. I have been very diligent and studious and have taken every advantage of the learning process. I have met many of the people who watch and guide you. They have been most kind to me and I am so grateful. My strong link with you and our harmonious vibrations brought me into line with them. They have taught me a great deal.

Your, Mrs Billie Campbell[52] is a character. I do like her so much. She and her husband, Donald, have been very hospitable to me and I really feel at home in their abode. We have some great musical evenings. They are very interested in Giles. Really, it is very amusing to us because we hear you and Chris getting annoyed with Giles because he doesn't go for a singing lesson but he's having them all the time – from us! Often when you tell him off for staying in bed at weekends – he's really with us, learning about singing. We have a grand time with him. He's a good sort and got a grand sense of humour. We all get on so well and often have a good laugh at your expense 'cos you're so intense. You

---

[52] My last singing teacher but I had no idea that her nickname was Billie.

are a worrier, you know. You may not think it and it all comes from being so conscientious, but you could unwind more and have a bit more fun. You take everything so seriously.

Regardless of what you do or don't do, he will fit into his own pattern. All the major posts are marked up along the way for him. Are you so sure university is for him? There are some good music colleges too, you know.[53] However, just let things unfold in their own way. He has become much more studious and will impress in his interview to anyone who really knows his stuff. It's early days yet; he has a long way to travel and will do well. Just let him expand in his own way and his own good time. I know you both want to do your best by him but you've already done that in the way you've brought him up. All credit to you. He will be well thought of very early on and make his mark amongst the 'egg heads', though never an 'egg head' himself. His scope is wide – just let him develop and experience it. He will bring harmonious groups together and be quite a leading light.

Anyway, besides you, he has two excellent teachers in Billie and Donald and I do my best to keep him happy too, singing him some of the less erudite songs, those with a swing in their step to balance all the serious stuff he deals in. Just make sure he also has enough fun. It is easy to get carried away with absorbing subjects, as you know. Billie is very pleased with the way you've adapted to all the things that have been thrown at you and still kept your singing up. She thinks the voice sounds lovely and says the less you worry about it, the better. Just know, whenever you have to do anything in public, that you're supported and all will go well – again, that word 'trust'. You've put in all the hard work – now enjoy it. Maria Callas links with us because it was she who found Billie for you. She was alerted to you in 1980[54] and had to look around for a while to get someone to take you to Billie, who was literally under your nose at Wigmore Hall.[55] She was brought to your attention several times but you, silly little donkey, did not snatch the carrot. It took two years to get you to her and then you almost didn't turn up. It was known that her time (on earth) was short, yet she was the right person for you in so many ways. Maria thinks very highly of her.

I have met many people who've come over here knowing you. Harold Rosenthal[56] is a really nice man. I like him immensely and find him a mine of

---

[53] A year later Giles sat the entrance exam for Oxford but in the meantime was offered a scholarship to the Royal College of Music in London, which he accepted.

[54] When Mrs. Campbell taught at Wigmore Studios in London, Donald was her baritone husband whom she met as a girl when they were studying with the same teacher in Italy.

[55] Later, I realised that I had twice passed her on the stairs at Wigmore Studios but didn't know who she was, then I found out that Chris's WNOC colleague, Malcolm Williams, studied with her.

[56] He was a well-known music critic, who founded Opera Magazine with Lord Harewood. His wife, Phyllis, was a former student of Jillian Skerry and they were all great friends, which is how I met them. He was also a dear friend of Maria Callas and when she died, Phyllis said that it was the only time she had seen him cry.

information on opera. He is never too busy to spare time to instruct me, and I am learning and enjoying so much. I was a much better musician than I gave myself credit for, being a real natural. I could have soon got to grips with the technical side of music if I'd put myself to the trouble. I could have done as you did – go to the library and consult books.

I've been a musician in other lives and it was all there to be uncovered but I completely missed the boat, Neddy that I was. I could have had a fascinating life but I limited myself and was completely to blame for my frustrations. Yes, I had a family and had to support them but that needn't have held me back – others have triumphed over such things, so could I. I was idle, that's the simple answer; if it didn't come easily, I left it alone. Of course, such a lot of things did come easily in my singing and I thought that only right, instead of getting on with it and developing those gifts. Well, never mind, too late to alter that now, but I'm certainly making up for lost time, I can tell you.

I still see Cis and George from time to time and Harry, but gradually we settle into our own interests and gravitate to people of similar mind. I'm in my element now.

Well, how's this for name dropping – I've become familiar with Schubert. He is a fine teacher and still retains his inherent joy in singing and song. Of course, he is further developed from where he stood on earth, yet he is still the basically simple, loveable soul he was then, absolutely no side, but a true and great Master of Music. Well, my love, I think I've stolen a march on you. How's that for your old Dad's progress then?

Mind you, I appreciate how you've come on yourself. The kids you teach really love you. Never feel you don't know enough. You know plenty but the important thing is the love you give out – that is what they come for and what they feel. You fill them with warmth and love and they're devoted to you. You are putting so much their way which will serve them well in life, whether they take up music seriously or just for the fun of it. Keep up the good work and don't let it worry you. You're doing fine and your piano playing will improve if you just stick at it.

Must go love; I'm putting a vast input of power through you so I have to take care – don't want you to bust a gasket. Give my love to your mum. I am free of her now. I'm no longer tied as a prisoner. My feelings towards her are healthy and all is well. I no longer have the obsessive feeling of guilt but see her as an individual with whom I shared a mutual path in the course of experience. She and I still have much in common and I look forward to introducing her to all the varied elements of music and people I am discovering. She also limited herself and could have been a fine pianist coping with more advanced music, but also with producing a better standard of the stuff she actually performed; however, she thought she was OK as she was. Well, when she comes here, she'll see there don't have to be limitations; you can go as far as you like and further.

Your friend, Joan,[57] is a fine woman. I like her very much and we often meet and have a chat and a laugh. You seem surprised to think I know her as she's still on earth. Well, you know the importance of sleep state and the exchange of energies we have between planes – well, she comes here for the music. She's a really good soul who's had it hard but who keeps on trying – God bless her. She's fond of you and Chris. You should try and see her a bit more. She'd appreciate that.

Yes, I have met your Mrs Auerbach;[58] another very lovely person and with a decided mind of her own. She's very much into animals but sometimes comes to receive training from Schubert.[59] She loves the lied and is very up in German poetry. She's promised to help me so I can sing some of his songs in the original language but I don't think I am up to it yet – give me time – but nice of her to offer. She sometimes brings some of her animals to concerts. Don't laugh, it's true! They sit, good as gold, and soak it up. I know it sounds daft but it really is true – we're more democratic here than on earth and if wild or domestic animals want to come to concerts – so be it – they're welcome and really derive great comfort and blessings from the sound. It lulls them and removes any remaining aggressive streaks brought over from earth.

Well, I've used up most of the time and I haven't said much about your book. I know you are guided by those wiser than I. Yes, be honest, without being too long-winded about how it all came about. Maria certainly deserves the credit. She is the catalyst – along with your friend Christine.[60] There are many who deserve credit in your development but those two were really active in the field. If they hadn't been able to wake you up, many others would have missed out. As Ralph would say, 'you ain't seen nuffing yet'. You may think you've helped quite a few but you'll help many more in the years remaining to you. Yes, the printed word still holds sway. You will reach more through the book than you possibly could of yourself and there'll be other books to follow.[61]

I send my love to the family. I do not come home now but know through my 'crystal ball' how all is going on. There have been some traumas but they're none the worse for it because they are learning. All is well, don't doubt it. They'll get by and the more they can do of themselves, the better. It is not good for one's growth to be constantly helped out by others. Yes, lend a helping hand, of course; service is a lovely thing, but do not take command. There is so much we could

---

[57] A mezzo soprano who engaged me and Chris for opera performances in London schools

[58] Hilde Auerbach was my German teacher at the Guildhall School of Music and Drama in London

[59] She was a good pianist and highly cultured Jewish woman who escaped from Germany in 1938.

[60] Christine Holohan is the gifted clairvoyant who I have always called Christina.

[61] I hesitated to publish Dad's letters because I thought I would be ridiculed by my professional colleagues. Instead, I wrote two volumes of biography about the French 19th singer, Pauline Viardot Garcia. However, without the input of Maria Callas these would never have been written.

discuss but truly I have to break off for your own good. I will be back, never fear. All love, Your own adoring Dad.

As a young singer, I was ambitious but though I had a good career and was fortunate to earn my living by doing what I most enjoyed, I never became famous. However, Maria explained that I didn't need to go down that road because I had already experienced fame in my past incarnation. It can be a poisoned chalice and not all that people expect, but the purpose of my present incarnation is to progress spiritually, using music as the tool. There is a lot of disappointment and rejection even in the best of careers but if one stays the course, it is character building.

3rd November 1988

Hello, Barb, sorry you've been feeling down. Most people feel the effect of winter's advance. You have become particularly sensitive to these vibrations and this is why you feel the nihilistic effect. It's because you are tuning into the cessation of natural forces as they go into abeyance and lie dormant before the next phase of activity.

Your mum is OK; don't worry. She's really alright – there's nothing sinister; just your imagination proving false. No more worrying, OK? Don't say anything to Mary or you'll have her worrying too and it's unnecessary. Anyway, the doings at home are their business and they'll sort it out. Your mum loves company and it gives her some purpose, having meals to get and somebody to chat to and watch TV with. Also, she gets help with her shopping. Don't worry about money – they'll pay their way and there'll be a bit extra for her. She loves a letter; it sets her up for the day. Give her my love and tell her I'm always thinking of and doing my best to keep an eye on her.

Mary is fine; she has much to experience and will cope OK. She's a real little dynamo and won't be taken for a ride. Giles is doing well, isn't he? I told you he would with such fine teachers around him, plus his own abilities, of course. Don't worry about Chris. There are always reasons for the slack times as well as the active ones. You both have a lot to offer so you can't be allowed to trot off yet. You still have a course to run. Keep your pecker up and know you're not alone. Just call on me when you need a bit of company and support. You know I'm not far away – you felt my touch on your shoulder today, didn't you? Yes, it was me. I felt so sorry for how lost and weary you seemed. You'll pick up in a few days but remember, the natural forces are withdrawing so that is what is affecting you.

Music is a lovely thing, isn't it? How you picked up once you started singing. You see, it is your life – you are like a bird – it doesn't have to have an audience – it sings because it must – it is a feature of a bird's life. Well, if someone hears it and enjoys it, that's fine but it isn't necessary – it's a by-product. So it is with you – lovely to perform but almost incidental. You sing to keep healthy and you contribute to life's energies. Also, you help the kids to develop themselves and their own gifts and that way you learn too. Do not denigrate the role of a teacher. It is crucial to your own development. I know it's no good saying, cheer up and get on with it but truly, you are not alone – help is all around you. I can feel it. Just call on it and ask. I know you do but you don't trust it enough. Just plod on and remember all the times in the past when you've been sustained and helped. You are a silly billy at times. When in doubt, go back to your own notebooks and remind yourself of all the wonders you've experienced. If you hadn't, you wouldn't have been able to help others have their own experiences and to develop in their individual ways.

Yes, Ralph is fine. Always busy, always interested but not particularly caught up in worldly matters. He is developing his own way of life and experiencing loves from previous lives. He is not only tied to Sheila,[62] though at this stage she is to him but later she'll also discover those she has loved in other lives. When she comes here, she will be on an expanded level. This is something she will experience in her discarnate state, but at present, she cannot think in this way; she is not ready. Give her time. Ralph will not desert her but he has a much wider vista to cover and she cannot be allowed to hold him all to herself as she wants to do. He has to find the strength to free himself from her hold.

All this may sound callous but I think you understand what I mean. In earthly terms it is difficult to grasp but it relates to 'unconditional love'. Anyway, he keeps an eye on Sheila but she has to build up her own strengths, as he does, and she is lucky to have the boy.[63] He was given to her for a purpose. He has been her father in a previous time and is here to look after her once more until she is ready to stand on her own feet. I know it seems hard from her angle but we see so much more of intrinsic meaning and so are not put out by these things as you are.

Of course, I am a much more tolerant and feeling person now than I once was. My own suffering in my immediate post mortem state has encouraged this new attitude in me. This is why I felt so moved by how you were feeling this morning. I have tried to attract you to open spaces with trees because I knew I could get to you more easily and you see, you even felt my touch as though it were physical, and yes, I could see you.

Now, my darling, I'll let you go. I've supplied you with my energy. Now allow your own energies to gush forth. We're back to the old word 'trust', trust and you will experience your friends and teachers – you block yourself from them. There will be a fine power of healing here this evening and many will benefit from it. Your teachers are ready to manifest whenever you feel strong and ready enough to let them through. Don't doubt; you know in your true heart that it is not all of you. Of course, you have your part to play and are able to manifest them because you give of yourself – it is a truly co-operational feat. You know you need them but without you, they cannot produce a physical effect. Of course, you provide a base and the bias will be of your condition of thinking. This is as it should be. Without that there would be no link. Because you are what you are, you link with those of like mind. There has to be an absolute twinning. The vibrations and frequencies have to match completely then there is fusion.

---

[62] Ralph's wife
[63] Tim, their adopted son

So, my dear girl, get on with the precious work. When you come over, we two will be so much closer than we ever were on earth. I am so glad you are my daughter; nothing can ever cancel that out – even if our relationships change in future times. One day when I have found out more myself, we'll talk of past lives and experiences – surely we will but at present, I am dealing with other things.

You know I am thoroughly wallowing in music and it is rather different to what you have to go through on earth. Rather easier from my angle. I only have to think and desire music and can pick it from the air, just as people on earth pick fruit from a tree. I don't have to take exams – not yet, anyway. I am just enjoying the freedom to experience music to the full. I am also being given the opportunity to see music as both a creative and a negating force. This is why I am able to tell you about your sensitivity to the departing energies. It is not really depressing because though I see the shutting down of those energies – I see the build-up of the creative ones to come, which will bring about your spring. It is an illusion this running down of energy; really it is just a cross-over of vibrations.

For the work to come, you will both need to be very strong. That is why you are tested – just in the way that steel is tempered, rather than as an exam. Well, my dears do try to live for the day and not try to see too far ahead. It gives you a feeling of anxiety and is not necessary. All comes to you in its own good time. I do love you so, more now than ever because I understand you so much better than I ever did.

My heart overflows with pity and love when I see the struggles of many individuals on earth. I do wish to give service and help to them, and if I just bring a little flower to them or a sunbeam, I know I've done something to uplift and enlighten them in however small a degree. We shall do wonderful work together through music when you come here. Just hold on to that and believe it. Truly when you see from where I stand, you'll find it all worthwhile. The universe is vibrant with life; there's nothing nihilistic about it and when you are in need of a rest and a recuperative period deep inside your own soul, you are able to withdraw until such time as you feel ready to join the band once more. This is why we recommend that you relax and rest on earth and do not continually drive yourselves. Remember, all is rhythm and your service will be of more value when you are strong in yourself.

I am withdrawing but know I've not gone far, and can always be with you if you need me.

Chapter Thirteen
Stage Fright

Surprisingly after so many years on the stage and concert platform, I had begun to suffer badly from stage fright. This is a phenomenon that happens to many performers in the middle of their careers, even Sir Laurence Olivier, who was frightened of forgetting his lines. It takes great courage to go out and face the public when you are paralysed with fear. What makes it so terrifying is that it is not logical: it comes out of the blue and cannot be rationalised. There was one concert in particular, for which I was booked a year ahead, for a work I had already sung and which presented no vocal difficulties. It was nonsensical to feel terrified, yet it was as if every fear I had ever had or was likely to have, surrounded this concert. After meditating, I realised that it was a test of facing fear itself; I could overcome it, or it would appear in different forms. Somehow, the night before I felt very calm and the next day everything went well. Then I knew that I would never be as frightened again because I had come through the test. From that time, I began to enjoy performing again whether on stage, in the studio or broadcasting.

15th November 1988
Comfort from Maria.

My dear One, How could you think that I would desert you? My essence is always with you, though I am now in a non-physical state. Yet I haven't forgotten what it is like to live on earth and to suffer. Know that anything you suffer, I have also felt. Yes, I too have been frightened and overcome by nerves to a tremendous extent. It was not so in my earlier days but became so later when the press were on my tail.

You do not have the weight of such a reputation to consider; therefore go forward and enjoy the act of singing. It is a wonderful therapy you know, and to be enjoyed, not feared.

You have no need to worry about your concerts, I shall be with you. Remember how I was able to help you with Pamina. Well, so it will be again and you'll be conscious of my presence and know I am with you.

Believe me when I say you no longer sing for yourself and your own satisfaction but are used by the sons and daughters of Light to bring peace. Of course, you are one among many but you are dear to us because you have come through many trials and have accepted and overcome all that has been meted out to you.

Now comes the interesting part. Because you have proved such a good channel, I shall be able to sing once more on the earth plane. I shall sing through you – I use your voice and your means in a physical sense. I will not override you or possess you. Truly, it is a divine partnership, planned by your soul and mine long before we took on the earthly forms of Maria and Barbara.

We link on many levels but the last incarnation was crucial to us. We have long loved singing and music and so it goes on.

I am delighted with the way you have handled the singing lessons. Your students are indebted to you, not least because of the love and kindness you have shown them.

It is humble work but you have applied yourself devotedly and so much merit has been gained in this way.

You do not need to berate yourself because of your lack of proficiency in playing the piano.[64] It makes your pupils laugh when you stumble and stops you appearing superior to them. You become one of them, also learning, and in that way, you do not inhibit them.

Now, my dear sister and friend, you do well to concentrate on healing, not just physically, but morally, spiritually and emotionally. You cannot lose out by putting the needs of another before your own, believe me.

We have come such a long way together in the past few years. Just because you no longer see me in my last physical guise, do not be upset; know I am with you and whenever it is necessary, I will send you a mental 'post-card', as I did today, so you will know. [65]

I have to contact you from a higher/finer vibration so that I link in on a different frequency. In previous times, I was closer to the earth vibration and could enter your home. Now it's like being on closed-circuit TV but none the less potent for that. In fact, it gives me a wider perspective.

I will bring my expertise for your disposal. We all love you; never forget that and there are many who are grateful to you for what you did for them in your last incarnation. That is why you have so many linking with you and taking an interest from this side.

I like your father – he is a dear soul and so humorous. He will be taking an interest in all you do.

When all has been given up and taken away, all can be given back again – with interest. You can tell that to your friend Wendy. She will not lose out but is sorely tested at present. With your help, she'll pull through and acquire greater strength, Maria.

---

[64] I never practised enough.

[65] It would appear that a kind of holographic system is used to convey pictures to the earth. White Feather said that this uses a lot of energy so like a child who has outgrown picture books, I did not need to receive visions but would know telepathically and intuitively what was intended.

24th November 1988
From my father:

Hello, Barb, Nice to be with you again. I see you're a bit tired so I won't stay too long but I do like to keep in touch. Your recital went better than you know. You have certainly built up a lot of strength now in your performances and they sound lovely, so soothing yet stimulating and producing a degree of courage and love in those who come to hear, as well as building up the atmosphere.

Your mum is keeping her pecker up and is pleased to have company in the house. She's not really one to enjoy being alone, so it's good that the others are still at home, although, of course, not for long.

She'll never be left alone for long. She's a good soul; even though she can be cantankerous at times and likes her own way. Anyway, she's all heart and that's all to the good, bless her.

Do try to get up over Christmas; she'd like that, so would Mary, as she can't be there much.

Ralph sends his love but won't bother you today. Just tell Sheila he loves her and give his best to Tim.

13th December 1988
Ralph makes direct contact with me.

Dear Coz, I must just take this opportunity while you have a quiet moment to send love to my dear Sheila and Tim. I'm sure you will not have much time for contemplation over Christmas, so I want them to know now that I shall be with them and thinking of them over the festive season.

Tell them to have a drink with me and a mince pie (I always enjoyed them) and I will do my best to let them feel my presence and to get a message to them via the (Spiritualist) Church. It doesn't get easier for Shie but she just gets on with it and doesn't ask any favours.

People don't realise how much she still cries inside because she puts on such a good front and I certainly am proud of her. Tim is beginning to develop his innate gifts and is increasing his consciousness of things 'unseen'. It takes a while and there are many and varied patches to go through but he's started off on the path and will surprise himself as the years go by.

I often join him in his thoughts. I love the way he works things out and I feel proud of him too, the way he's coped with life and all its limitations.[66] But now, everything is opening out for him and he'll see far more of the world, in every respect, than he ever thought possible.

The trips to Italy will resume – they must – we can't let our good friends down after all they've meant to us. Italy is a second home and I'm willing Sheila to get up the courage to go again. I will be there, don't doubt it. I often go and sit on the hillsides outside Genoa and re-live some of the marvellous times we've had there. I can link in with all those positive vibes of love and enjoyment from

---

[66] He was in an orphanage when Sheila and Ralph first met him.

my times there and it gives me strength and a great sense of wellbeing and pure pleasure. Say 'ciao' to them all for me.

I want Shie to know I'm often at her elbow and when there's peace and quiet, I can really tune in with her.

It's sad that there had to be a parting but really the parting is only an illusion and the reunion will set the world ablaze!!!

The more they can lift themselves up from the daily chatter and trivia and turn into the quiet, tranquil centre of themselves, the more they will contact me. It has to come about in peace and quiet; there can be no contact in the mad bustle of the world but when it is quiet, I draw near and stand beside them and pour my love into their hearts and auras and they know something lovely has happened to them.

Draw near, my dear ones. I cannot make your decisions for you or influence you. You have to live your own lives but I can give you my peace and tranquillity and above all, my love, to make you strong.

Keep on, my dears, and love me as I love you, unceasingly and always.

Enjoy your Christmas, no long faces – no regrets. All is as it should be. God bless you. All my love, Ralph(ie).

3rd January 1989

Dear Coz, Many thanks; won't keep you long – just wanted you to tell Sheila that I'm delighted at how things are going. She does my heart good to see her courage and the way she's coping. As she links with others in distress, she will see how privileged she has been and what a wealth of comfort she will bring to them.

She and Tim will work together because their energies complement each other and both are necessary, with two halves making a whole.

This will really show up at a later date. It's early days yet but they've taken to it like ducks to water and it's great that they are getting so much from it. Also, I can keep an eye on them as it's easier for me to hold their vibrations now they've linked to the Spiritualist Church because of the combined energies and light which is stimulated there.

Sheila was dubious when I said we'd link 'face to face' but it's becoming more possible and the more disciplined she is, and less emotional, the stronger our ties will be.

There is a great depth of healing energy to be plumbed and it will gradually emerge. It has to come through slowly as it is always a two-edged sword and these energies can be dangerous if unleashed before the body has built up sufficient insulation. They are very potent and in existence all the time but have to be directional to be of benefit in this individual way. This is a bit difficult to understand, no doubt, but very real.

My father then joined in: Bless you, Barb. A Happy and Prosperous New Year to you all. So glad you were able to be in Brum for a few days. Lovely to have you there and to know of the light you were able to pass on to our dear ones. They are not always easy to help but we have to keep trying. It is hard not to be insistent when you see how much they could help themselves but you know by now that we have to hasten slowly.

Good girl, do what you can but don't be too hard on them. Let them come along in their own time and on their own terms. There's little to add, duck. Glad you enjoyed the book.[67] Yes, a good two-thirds is my own work. It doesn't matter to me that I am not credited as an author. That sort of need is past. I am just pleased if others derive pleasure from it.

Everyone is pleased with Giles's trip.[68] He's doing a good job too. He's linking up with many forces of light and love and will make a big success with his singing. It goes right to the heart with nothing getting in the way. Allow it to flower unhindered. He will come to no harm. He is so well in touch with his Higher Self and more understanding will come forth with every year. This is not his first trip to Russia; he's known it in his past.

I cannot tell you more now but he will start to remember. He has made connections with past vibrations and in time his inner memories will be awakened. Keep well, my dear one. Love to Chris. He is making great progress.[69] Good for him. He is beginning to know his real values.

I'm sorry that Mary was upset because she felt that I hadn't mentioned her sufficiently. None of you are ever far from my thoughts and she must know how dearly I love her and all of you. I am so proud of her. My heart expands when I see all she's done and coped with over the years. She has a good heart and nothing can gainsay that – it is a precious gift. Her concern for the family has always been great; now it's becoming more balanced and is very valuable.

We all have hard lessons to learn. It is not easy when you have a tender heart to let people be. It is always a case of trying to do more but just giving moral support and a loving word does more than you know.

I feel frustrated that I cannot relate more; it is like trying to get everything over in a telegram. I try to link with you, Barb, but you're not always aware and have a lot on your plate. I'll keep in touch; never fear. Just sit quietly when you can because even if I can't put over to you all I would like to say, at least we can warm ourselves by each other's fire and link in love and well-being

Your mum is a dear soul and does try, even when she finds it difficult. Don't let a day go by without sending her light – it will uplift and strengthen her so much. She's thrilled when you tell her how much she means to all of you. Lay it on with a trowel because it's meat and drink to her. You all mean so much to her and it is the best thing in her life to know how much you need and love her.

Tell them to bury all hatchets. Forget trivial quarrels and criticisms. Have a good laugh – look on the bright side and remember all the good times, of which there have been many. We've had some great laughs as a family, even during

---

[67] *Up the Terrace*, by Ronald K .Moore, Westwood Publications, 1988, for which Albert provided a large amount of material in the last year of his life.

[68] Giles was then eighteen years old and sang *Ich Habe Genug* by Bach with Paul Sartin, oboe, in the Hall of Columns in Moscow on a trip to Russia with fellow students from the Purcell School of Music as part of a cultural exchange between young musicians.

[69] When Dad talks of progress, he usually means on a soul level.

traumas and rows. Take joy in one another. I see a lot of good things coming up for all of you, Steve[70] included. It's like watching the sun come up over the horizon.

Just keep your chins up. Mary has so many doors opening; she'll have a job running from one to the other but like a good juggler, she'll manage to keep all the balls in the air. How's that for a mental picture?

Now, about the book, Barb,[71] it is meant to go ahead. Don't be despondent if it's not snapped up at once but keep plugging away and know it will find its mark in time. I'm sorry I can't advise you in more detail. It would seem logical to offer you a publisher and see it all plain sailing but it doesn't work like that. It is part of the plan that you should learn by your own searching.

By the way, I think you can tell your friend Vera that all is going to work out well.[72] She'll never know how much her own 'good behaviour' has helped the case (*a forthcoming divorce*). She could have rocked the boat but she hasn't. Things could have been delayed but are working out well (*for March*). I wish I could say the same for some others of your 'cases'. Never mind, they'll learn by it but could save themselves heartache.

I am very interested in your 'little band',[73] as well as wider acquaintances. I feel what truly loving people they are.

I'd love to go on but see your time is limited. Don't forget to tune in again soon – as all the best DJ's say. What a broadcasting station we've got – beats the World Service hands down.

22nd March 1989

Darling Barb, lovely to link again. Long time since you did this work in this way. I'm glad to assist. I know you get little time to yourself but if you keep to a commitment and link at the same time each week, you'll find the path cleared for you (*Chris and Barbara began performing in Arena Operas from 1988 until 1995, which took them as far as Japan as well as the UK and Europe*). It is necessary to have a regular time in order to carve a channel and the 'powers that be' will see you are not disturbed.

Giles will be occupied with friends and activities over the holiday and you will have peace and quiet. It is not the amount of time but the quality which counts; a lot can be achieved.

Well, there is much that we could talk about but first I'd like to comment on the girls.[74] It's a sad situation this eating or rather lack of it. Again many levels are involved and the best thing you can all do is to send love. Do not condemn or criticise; that merely sets up conflicting vibes. Quiet, warm, caring love is the best healer of all. You cannot go wrong in sending love, unconditional love I

---

[70] Mary's son

[71] Of his 'post mortem letters'

[72] She had discovered that her husband's secretary was expecting his child so a divorce was pending.

[73] The meditation group

[74] His granddaughters were developing anorexia

mean, and praying for whatever is best for the person concerned. Many lessons are learned the hard way, I know. I was stubborn and arrogant and caused myself much pain but boy, have I learned.

Now, with regard to my progress, I have undergone all sorts of things. At one and the same time, I have experienced heaven and hell. You see, we come over with a package of experiences, our harvest if you like. However, it is not that simple because we've lived other lives and we are also linked with those, so the karmic threads[75] are very relevant and we attract patterns which we've carved in the past.

We have areas of achievement – those parts where we've been truly loving and caring; the little kindnesses, the altruistic actions where we have overcome self; the higher aspirations. Opposed to those are areas of underachievement; less than worthy desires and things that still have to be worked out, having formed a karmic fluid, as it were. I had many unworthy fantasies to overcome, yet at the same time, I had high spiritual and musical ideals, so you see, it's quite a mishmash and not at all easy to deal with.

Nevertheless, one is given a lot of help if one looks for it and accepts it. I think it fair to say, I have balanced the sexual bit. It is really a creative drive and push towards evolution but not understood as such. The Kundalini energies can be very powerful, and if not handled well, activate too strong a sexual drive. If one's partner cannot match that drive, one has either to become promiscuous or to fantasise. Used properly that force is capable of producing masterpieces of art or scientific marvels, yet to most of us, they simply represent libido. We cannot reproduce all the time so the energies turn in on themselves; the sexual urge becomes predominant and an end in itself. I was unaware of this, of course, and was deeply unhappy within myself, yet there was seemingly little I could do about it so went along with it, considering myself a highly sexed chap, frustrated and unfulfilled.

Now I see that I could have achieved wondrous things by the application and use of those energies. Just applying them in sexual fantasy dissipated them and blocked the energy channels.

The intestinal cancer was linked to an imbalance of the lower frequencies. The eyesight problem was a psychological blockage because of what I did not want to see in myself, my life or others. Jealousy also ate away at my soul; not any one particular jealousy, more of lots of little ones; mostly pretty trivial really. However, they are deadly and bring forth poisons in the system, causing the trapped energies which lead to hardening of arteries and heart disease. Any negative energy stored in the body is dangerous and needs to be transmuted, so that positive energies can replace the negative ones: thus unifying the entire system, comprising mind, body and spirit. So you see, I've had a great deal of work to do on myself. It has occupied a deal of my 'time'.

I have had many delightful experiences too and singing has been my salvation. I have made good friendships with musicians and music lovers.

---

[75] Karma is a Sanskrit word loosely translated as action regarding sowing and reaping.

Classes are given by the 'angels of music' whose work is devoted to bringing forth patterns in sound that we call music. I also benefit from the creative world in general. Unlike you, I do not only hear music, I see it in intricate and beautiful patterns of colour, light and shade – and I am learning something of what you would call a science of sound. I am responsible for your own recent interest in sound as an energy and healing force. The finest music is more than entertainment; it touches the soul and promotes healing.

You see, at one and the same time, I have indulged all these deep desires brought over from earth. Even the negative ones, which I enjoyed, such as smoking, remain until we've become satiated and no longer require them. It's like burning it out of the system. This, I suppose, is one's personal refiner's fire. All the dross gets burned out and only the gold remains.

The purely physical desires (yes, we still feel them) can hold us in thrall and it is maddening to have these desires and not be able to assuage them. That is real hell and the heavy drinkers and drug addicts suffer most, although any addiction or craving brings suffering. The more you can jettison such things whilst in the body, the more beautiful and worthwhile you will find life here.

I am very busy creating myself a beautiful living area; a special place is necessary for all of us and the things we've held most dear can be gathered there. I have pictures in my mind's eye of you all, my dear ones still on earth, and I have peopled my place with you. I still hear you sing, Barb, and your mum play. I love Mary and Sue's sense of humour and I try to comfort the girls[76] and get them to see sense, reminding them that they have worthwhile lives ahead, so not to throw them away.

I try to impress on Tim[77] the value of loving behaviour and not to be so headstrong and thoughtless. Of course, I can only impress; I cannot and would not dictate to any of you but with my new expanded field of love and my newly acquired knowledge, I do try to bring my influence to bear. I love my family and am so proud of Steve and Giles and all of you. I am pleased too to have such good lads as sons-in-law.

Bless you all, darlings; know you are never out of my thoughts and join me mentally whenever it all gets too much for you. Remember, you need peace and refreshment. My special place is very lovely; beautiful scenery, lots and lots of flowers, trees, lakes and waterfalls, also many birds and animals. I love the song of birds and am learning so much from them. I do interact with many on my own plane. The thing I like so much is that you are always with your own kind. If you are not too highly evolved you are with others of like kind. There is no competition but as you develop, you co-operate more with each other.

We are visited by higher beings and they guide and influence us because this is how evolution works[78]. If left to ourselves with only our own kind, we might

---

[76] Neither of the girls could defeat anorexia and the younger one died when she was twenty-six, the older one when she was thirty. Both girls were exceptionally beautiful and had devoted boyfriends but the addiction to weight loss was too strong.

[77] Dad's youngest grandson

[78] I presume he means spiritual evolution.

never make a move but we become aware of other lights, more beautiful, perfumed and expressing such love that we want to follow them. That is how we rise up and grow larger than ourselves. Each time we have a higher aspiration, of course, we are linking more strongly with the Higher Self, and in that way we expand, then each expansion brings forth the next. Gradually, we leave aside the tawdry toys we have thought so necessary and reach upwards to higher and better things. We are not badgered but when we send out a call with a desire for something better, it is answered and the teacher appears. Never doubt the strength and love of these teachers. You on earth are also linked with them. As you become ready for further teaching or as you call out to be allowed to help and to heal, your calls are always heard and always responded to. Your answer may come in unexpected ways, though you may not approve of the methods employed. However, the teachers are older and wiser and know what is needed.

You are tested very strongly and potently, as we all are. The intensity of your desire to progress, the strength of your commitment, your tenacity and your ability to express unconditional love; all of these things the teacher has to ascertain and so you are challenged as to the seriousness of your intent. If you put to good use what is given to you, more will follow. You also experience fallow periods which you baulk at. However, only in that way is the soil prepared for further growth. So you see, all is really on the upward spiral, though you don't always realise it. Keep to your path, even when things don't work out. As long as you've done your best and you are being true to yourself and to others, just sit tight, refusing to despair; then see how things are re-arranged. You cannot at your present stage or I at mine, know all the pros and cons. Trust is the most important word in the dictionary. Keep love flowing in your hearts and know you'll never be overlooked. The Universe will treasure every act and thought you have which will increase its evolution and will gladly and willingly accept all you have to give from a loving heart.

I have been able to pass over more than I had expected. Your rest has done you good, Barb. Remember the importance of regularity and commitment and know that I respond to your love.

For a while I had been mentally questioning why there was so much evil in the world and on the 20th of April, 1989, I received the following answer.

The 'dark force' holds and limits. It oppresses. It organises in a restricted way. When unleashed, it is highly dangerous and potentially lethal. It is the Dragon force – the Beast. It was the force unleashed by Nazism and created the Youth, the Military and the secret Societies which generated the Concentration Camps.

It was also unleashed in Russia over the centuries, imposing restrictions, the imposition of Serfdom; imprisonments and the KGB purges. It is seen in all places where men cannot think freely and wherever there is imprisonment without justification. It is the antithesis of the light force which enlarges, embraces, which soars and which encourages growth.

Yet, the dark force is a form of primal earth energy and is allied to the Cosmic force which breaks down and changes the nature of matter, enabling the creative force to produce further forms. It is an aspect of Cosmic rhythm but in its earthly manifestation can create perversion.

If man is unbalanced in himself and his environment, it is easy for the dark force to be unleashed and results in mayhem. It is the genie out of the bottle and it is almost impossible to put back again, as in the case of war. Another analogy is Pandora's Box, the opening of which filled the earth with disease and all manner of dangerous things.

The myth of Adam and Eve and original sin goes back into far antiquity, way beyond the Bible and tells of intelligences of a more advanced system unwittingly invoking the dark force with which they were unable to deal. Adam was kept ignorant of its presence but curiosity overcame him and Eve and they unleashed the symbolic Serpent. However, sometimes a serpent signifies wisdom. Naturally, this story is simplistic but represents humanity in an early stage of spiritual evolution.

When this force has been unleashed, the only remedy is the solvent of Unconditional Love. That is why the great teachers always taught the necessity of forgiveness. Loving the enemy is extremely difficult for any human being but it is the only way to overcome the mindless, destructive, violent force.

In a perfect world, there would not be destruction, only the transmutation of energies into new vibrations when previous ones had run their course.

Anyone who would restrict and limit a fellow human in whatever degree is in danger of unleashing this force.

On the 27th April 1989, there was advice for those who felt drawn to be Light Workers.

Hold to all that you know and trust despite anything negative around you. The forces of darkness would hold back the Light; only your own light within can illumine you at these times. Keep strong and know that outside of time the Light is sublime and heavenly, and divine beings exist and live in the Godhead.

They are truly there and cannot dissolve or go away, yet on earth, you are surrounded by darkness. Whenever the Light is streaming forth, the dark forces do their best to cut off the beam. Only by your integrity and trusting what you know will the link hold.

Do not let your heart become heavy because that defeats the object and brings forth trouble and woe. Know that the testing is not of the Light, but of the darkness. Having come this far, do not give way to it or enter into earthly disputes.

Stand clear, stand on your mountain and survey the scene you have traversed. Stay in the clear, pure air, away from the machinations of the earth plane where there is pain and gnashing of teeth. You know what you know; you are what you are. Therefore, you will come up against darkness. You are light and the darkness abhors light and would put it out.

You stand on a precipice and your hold is tenuous but you have inner strength and there are powers above and beyond those of darkness. They will help you to hold your position as long as you are true. Your own integrity is the link. Stay firm with what you have overcome; do not give in to the 'little self' with its selfish wants and petty squabbles.

As you are able to hold your position, the darkness will be vanquished and a further display of light will come forth to astound and astonish the earth plane. Light workers will be multiplied from the Planes of Harmony.

Do not look for form; we are beyond form; the higher the frequency into which you tune, the nearer you connect to the Godhead (*The Elohim, the guardians of humanity describe themselves as being just short of Godhead*). We are pure energy, pure love. It is hard that you are required to take all this on trust but your five senses are not designed to comprehend in the normal way. Humanity has to evolve further in order to fully understand. However, know that it is so.

You have traversed many worlds within the physical universe as well as Astral levels; now you are out in Cosmic space – far from the density which provides form (*Potentially, all human beings are multidimensional and often experience other levels during sleep*).

Keep your lines of communication open and call on us at any time; we hear; we are aware. We love you and will not leave you; yet you are so far away in vibratory state. Only as you raise and refine your consciousness will you draw close and experience us in our own environment.

Stay calm; be still and loving and you will draw near. Through your group and their aspirations, you will all draw nearer (*This was a regular meditation group that met at my house*). Your love and your concern for suffering humanity will not go unheard and the energies will go into the central store to be used as and where needed.

Accept our benediction – know all is well. Trust your healing – stop dwelling in darkness and know that the light will heal the flesh. Cast off despair and despondency and stand in the Light.

Keep positive, grow strong in your light and watch your life and the everyday world take on a new hue. Pain (*a back injury*) has limited you. It does not need to – it can enhance, uplift and expand you. You have nestled your energies and drawn them closer to you. Now let them soar. Enough of pain and illness; it has brought a certain amount of learning and understanding, now let compassion come forth and a truly new dispensation will lead you onward into the next phase of learning and working.

In August 1989, I experienced an inner loneliness which I queried; this was the message I received:

We are with you, never doubt; however often you feel alone and bereft. That we are attached to you is an indisputable fact. It has always been so, it will always be so. We are all one! You link where you have affinity; there is no separation in a living, breathing, creative world.

All are experiencing on behalf of The One. Life is eternal and glorious. Your position is hard won.

Fear is a part of learning and experiencing. As you overcome it, you will be brought further into the Light. Without fear, you could not learn about negative vibrations and they are as important as the Light, being part and parcel of the Whole.

Now you will understand those who also suffer. Only as you experience and overcome fear can you grow in wisdom. You are not adventurous enough. You play safe, yet life is nothing if not an adventure. The whole Cosmos is adventuring. It does not play safe, if it did, it would disintegrate and die but it is dynamic and ever learning and experiencing.

Give yourself freely to life and enjoy it. You are at present in a chrysalis stage. That is part of growth. There are cobwebs to be cleared and inner levels to touch. If constantly surrounded by people and activity you cannot touch inner space.

As plants grow they need darkness and warmth before emerging into the sun, so the soul needs time to assess and assimilate. It is all a natural part of rhythm and growth which you are now starting to recognise and accept.

A tremendous amount of progress has been made in a relatively short time and this is all to the good but has produced a certain shock to the system and has brought a need for further alignment. Do not worry, all is well and you will be looked after and not allowed to stray. Good luck is yours already but more is coming your way. The trip to France was postponed because it was not merely for the things you originally planned. Timing is always crucial and you will meet now those you would have previously missed. It is intended that you go with Jill (*my pianist and friend*); your lives run in parallel and there is much to be uncovered.

You have a lot to learn and it will fascinate you. You will be drawn to places because we guide you and it will help you to 'lay ghosts' and to tidy ends remaining from your previous earthly incarnation.

This information was prophetic as it applied to Jill as well as to me because apparently, we had shared a life together in France although we were unconscious of it.

On the 15th of May, 1990, I posed the question, "What is the relevance of Rosicrucianism today?"

As always, it is to hold the Light; to resurrect the flame and to bring forth Truth. It is apparent that the Truth is truly needed at this time. Many are stumbling and suffering – mayhem is abroad. Only those of knowledge can hold the balance; knowledge of the keener things of life is ever necessary. The inner world is a real world, not fantasy, as many imagine. It is an inside/outside universe. Your world is an illusion; that is no exaggeration. We have told you before of 'Alice Through the Looking Glass'. Your world has a certain kind of illusory realism and while you are denizens of this plane it holds you in its grasp and you believe that is all that there is. However, as you grow to 'man's estate' you become aware of the reality of the inner worlds. Thus you grow to know the real from the unreal; the temporary from the permanent. So, you lose the fear of death because you know all is life – all is continuous – interpenetrating, all life; all being.

Surely, you are aware of many worlds, many dimensions, many levels and areas of reality? So, you are a Rosicrucian; that is all it means, it is a fraternity of the Spirit. It cannot be gauged by a worldly society. It is a society ordained from primordial times. Only those who have reached a certain degree through many ages and cycles become members; yet, as they reach the relevant stage of degree they are automatically enrolled and the inner teaching takes on an outward form.

The earthly personality does not have a great deal to do with this stage which is engendered through many lifetimes. On an earthly level, the personality is necessary, yet it is a cloak over the true identity.

Even an Initiate has still a good deal to learn and much to overcome and develop; therefore a particular type of personality is created to serve those aspects more readily than another one would. The mask of personality is like a suit of clothes but is temporary. It is the individuality that is eternal.

The experience of each personality is gradually absorbed into the individuality or crumbles away, leaving only that which is of value to the permanent atom. Yet on Astral levels, an essence remains; a remnant which can be contacted by those still on earth if it can be of use to either of them.

In time, the Individuality progresses, grows and outshines its personalities. In aeons of time it outgrows the need for them. It has passed through all it needs of physical life and moves into areas of which you cannot conceive because you have no yardstick.

Yet, you have moved on beyond the merely astral planes and have touched the essence of your true and eternal home. That is the reason you sometimes awaken depressed or anxious. You have caught a glimpse of Paradise and nothing else will do. It is your soul's deep acknowledgement of the distance you still have to go and the realisation of the work you do which ties you to the lower worlds.

There is much afoot on your earth plane today. There is a great sifting and sorting out and humanity is trying to get its house in order. Though you are all individuals, humanity itself is an entity; the microcosm in the macrocosm and vice versa. When you move house you often experience chaos because you realise that you have hung onto and hoarded things that no longer serve you. Also, you discover dirt, dust and grit under carpets; behind furniture and cupboards which have to be cleared away. Many items have to be discarded but valuable things are kept for the new house. You settle down in a new area, adopt a new lifestyle, meet new acquaintances and make new friends leading to a new social network and circumstances.

On a larger scale, this is happening on earth because it is time for a shift in consciousness. People are being moved in numerous ways and tested as never before. Some are succumbing to depression, emotional and mental disorders as well as addictions and cannot find the strength or courage to float free.

Wherever you can engender a sense of optimism, bestowing healing and courage you give a service, not just to the individual but to society and the earth as an entity.

Few of you realise how indebted to the earth you are. You are lodgers on this plane, just travelling through. The earth has been patient in the extreme and few of you are model lodgers. You take liberties; you are dirty, unkempt, shaming the name of humanity. You discourage the earth yet she bears with you and tries to adjust and adapt herself to your depredations.

Each one of you who is able to rise above the general malaise and generate love for Mother Earth and her progeny gives her hope and heart, and in time your emanations of love will spread and will affect others because you are all linked by invisible chains. Only a few of you realise these links because the general attitude of separateness and selfishness is part of your illusion.

Keep to your path – stay strong in the Light then you will be of benefit to your kinsfolk. Never enter into dissension or argument; do not shout or enter political forums. Work from a quiet background and continue to broadcast love and healing on the ether. Emanation is a strong metal – unbreakable. Determine to stay as a Rosicrucian always should; in the background; in the shadows, yet surrounded by Light. All is well; go in peace.

The following reply was received on 4th June 1990, for someone who had asked for advice about their path in life.

Yours is the choice. You have given much valuable service for which we are grateful. You are now more at ease within yourself and casting a beautiful, beneficial light which will be used, never fear. Do not think that you have to carry everything single-handedly; your time is well occupied and we know the need for you to have more mental space and balance. It is understood and you are thanked. There will be other avenues of service. We know you will not give up the desire to serve and that you do so every day. We tried an experiment and it worked. Many have been helped by your efforts and it has spun off into other areas (through teaching).

Use your power of choice and centre yourself. Focus your energies and they will grow. You have indeed been drawn on many fronts and have not been found wanting. You have now reached the point of choice and can decide where you wish to place your energies. Your guides will now be changed but those who have worked with you in the past will still draw close. None of the knowledge you have acquired will be wasted because all will be used and channelled. As you commit yourself, so the wheels will turn.

You have been prepared to give up and sacrifice that which you loved so dearly and to which you have devoted your life. Because of your willingness, that which you sacrificed will be returned to you a hundredfold. Go back to your studies, work, and more will follow.

The fourth dimension has been reached and you can work there most advantageously. You consciously occupy two realms and nothing is wasted. You are valuable because your time is doubled. Go forth unhindered and let your inner self be your guide. In love and light, your Guardians.

I had been requested to publish the messages but had failed to do so for fear of ridicule; the following message refers to 'the book'.

It is necessary at this time for such books to come forth. There has been much erroneous teaching over the centuries but the reality is far simpler than the accepted teachings purport. The true solvent to cure all ills is love but humans have not understood the true nature of love which is the stuff of the Universe and unconditional.

As you are on earth so you will be on your transition (death) because all you can take with you is yourself – the inner core of your being (consciousness). Just as there are many different types of individuals, so there are varying forms of experience which await the on-going soul.

There is a good deal of diversity but within these writings, you are in touch with the Western culture – that of the East would give a different picture. Yet, underlying the varied cultural aspect is the Eternal Law. All receive their just deserts; there is no favour, only that which has been earned. Even the worst types will have many other chances. You are all embarked on a vast spiral journey; a journey to the stars and to your true ancestral home which is Union with the Everlasting Light.

Hold to the Light and keep your hearts full of love; know that all is moving ever onwards, changing yet unchanging.

The message on the 11th June 1990, was in answer to questions about the mystery of the prehistoric stone monuments found in the British Isles, France and in various places around the world. I have no scientific knowledge so cannot guarantee that I brought through the information accurately. However, I trust that it gives some idea of the principles involved.

It would be beneficial to have knowledge of electricity in order to understand the principles involved in this matter. The stone needles (menhirs) in alignment act as a connection in the power grid. In an electric fire, an element flows through a glass tube or metal coil. These are necessary to stabilise the excited electrons which bring the energy into manifestation as heat.

The Ancients knew how to use energy in many forms but what we are at present discussing, and let us keep it as simple as possible not trying to take in too much too soon, is to use the earth's natural telluric currents as you use a coil or glass tube in which to run the energy.

The stone needles set up a buzz and this is then generated and connected by the ley lines. It was found most efficacious to project and nourish that energy in straight lines of current.

Just as your civilisation is based on oil, so the earlier one, which was beyond 10,000 BC, was based on a more sophisticated mode than oil, though you could say that it, together with coal and gas, are a form of telluric energy because they are derived from the earth itself.

It was important that calculations were made to ascertain the times of eclipses because if people were travelling through the air on telluric energy via the ley currents an eclipse would possibly cause a diminution of the energy so that craft would fall out of the sky. Other accidents could happen as a result of the jamming of the system as when traffic lights break down.

At present, your civilisation has no idea of the high level of sophistication known in pre-historic times. All was based on true communion and was cooperative. The teachers of the race were what you would now term 'psychic' and were able to expand their consciousness into other realms and bring forth knowledge and wisdom from higher sources. The society was not purely a material one but was of a semi-physical mode though the later stone features are material. However, we are speaking of a time of great antiquity so the elements had not hardened to the degree you find today.

The civilisations under discussion belonged to the Atlantean Age and were followed by those of the present Aryan Age. The physical forms of the Atlanteans were very tall but the early members of the Aryan race were much shorter. The life spans of the Atlanteans were also much longer than those of the Aryans. The latter have gained in the use of dense and heavy material atoms. In time, other races will look back to your achievements and there have been many, despite the horrors of war and suffering.

There have been wonderful works of art, music and science in spite of the opposite side of the coin, and even in the worst of times, there have been acts of compassion, heroism and valour. This human race has had a difficult learning process but the 'messy' part is coming to an end and there will be a new dispensation of Light which will bring forth new truisms and levels of understanding.

As you have a great urge to know and learn in this area, we will help you.

There was apparently more information that could have been given but it was withheld because it could cause harm if it was misused by those who were not wise enough to handle it.

Many are searching and discovering fresh sources and facts, yet the time of revelation is not yet. The Earth will have to be more stable before such things are taught. You are no scientist so you have no vested interests. It is all to the good that in many cases your scientists are struggling and going round in circles. It keeps them out of mischief. So much harm has been done by the clever ones who lack wisdom or conscience.

We cannot interfere with free will, yet we do our utmost to conserve and bring forth emanations of love and wellbeing. That is all for this time.

The message received on 16th June 1990, had a religious connotation.

The 'New Dispensation' is of John, the earlier one was of Paul. The Pauline teachings have to give way to an understanding of the Revelations of John, the Divine. That is why the name John appears over and over again; it cannot be forgotten. It is of the moment and the future. It links that which has gone before and that which is to come. Not only the Pauline epistles but of an earlier race and time: that of which you have an interest – the higher knowledge of aspects beyond the present state of knowledge.

All has to be relearned over and over because there are always 'new' souls developing and they have to walk the same way and acquire the knowledge for themselves.

Humanity has been through a very 'messy' time for the past 2,000 years and cruelty and suppression have been rampant. Suppression is ever the tool of the unready and the ignorant. Overcoming such oppression and allowing the light of hope and altruism to shine through develops steel in the spirit of Man.

Many people at this time are going through torment due to the various suppressions caused through tyranny but it is indicative of the degree of spiritual evolution that they have reached. Send love and light to them because they need it. Do not allow yourselves to fall into the slough of despond. There is no need and truly this sifting has to take place. All is not as desperate as it seems seen from the level of physical life. As you rise above it, you begin to see the patterns forming which lead to the next big leap in evolutionary status. Thus, all goes according to plan. However, seen by individuals on a personality level, it looks and feels desperate but the material aspect you see is merely the tip of the iceberg because most of the battles rage between dimensions and densities.

The overcoming of the inner, hidden battles is of overwhelming importance. That is the real Armageddon and it is going on all the time. It is not something in the future; it has always been a part of the learning process on earth. The civilisation to which your mind is drawn had gone through that and had reached a high state of being; thus they had no further need of the school of earth. They graduated into the next level.

The survivors were those who had not made the grade in the evolutionary sense and stayed to begin the next term, as it were. Thus the knowledge was already being lost. They had not fully understood but remembered certain things. However, some of the knowledge remained and there have always been Guardians who have observed, monitored and taught those who were ready to learn. Nevertheless, the race as a whole was a new one and had to learn all over again.

8th July 1990

The Mystery teachings have ever been oral. In this way, each one accepts or otherwise to their capacity; all then remains fluid and dynamic – a living tradition. When things are written down, they are crystallised and eventually become the dogma of a 'dead' tradition. This you will know and understand from the various religions and the difficulties that arise from set tenets.

None of the great Teachers left written documents; those who supplied them were their followers and disciples. The knowledge could only be given to the level of their own understanding so that it is not the 'absolute' truth that it has been purported to be ever since.

However, if you wish to go ahead with your writing it will help to clarify things in your own mind, up to your own level, but make it quite plain in your teachings and as part of the evolutionary process of education, that there should be no crystallisation resulting in dogma. Truth is dynamic and ever expanding.

Many are having great struggles with materiality and many lessons have to be learned and experiences undergone; but the lessons are crucial and cannot be overlooked on a physical, dense planet such as this. These are not just lessons for the little personality but experience for the Spirit in order to fully manipulate matter and not be used or controlled by it. The largest test will come through computerisation; the danger is that man will give up his free will to machines and that is an extremely dangerous time.

Vastly ancient civilisations have foundered at this point; not, perhaps, in quite the form you find before you today, but certainly on the same principles. It is a situation of extreme delicacy. Ordinary physical health can be sacrificed on the altar of computerisation but also, the emotional, psychic realm is involved; as indeed is the Spiritual; where the Spirit has to strive to remain in charge of the personality and the physical life of the entity.

Free will is truly relevant; there can be no doubt but the context is wider than you are aware and does not just constitute the experiences of the conscious mind but of the deeply hidden part of the iceberg, the sub-conscious mind, which holds many spells and secrets, and to which is attached the Karmic seeds.

Enough for now; you have been given a good deal to consider. You asked for guidance and understanding – you have it. Just carry on. If there are students to benefit from your teaching, they will be brought to you. When there is no need for the present form of class; you will be notified of the change (*This was true as shortly afterwards an inner group was formed*).

Just keep on keeping on joyfully and know you are not alone. Just remain true. Over this past year, you too have grown in knowledge and will have more on which to draw. Go in peace and love.

Chapter Fourteen
Past Incarnations

In addition to receiving letters from my father, Ralph and others, I was, of course, involved with my work as a singer and teacher by which I earned my living. I did not receive payment for my spiritual work or healing.

25th March 1990

Telepathically, I asked my father: "Is there anything you would like to say about past incarnations and the connections in the family?"

Yes, there have been many times when we've been linked, sometimes in near relationships and others less so. Reincarnation is not quite so simple and it is not until you get out of incarnation that you have any real sense of what is actually involved. There are links with nearest and dearest and with friends and acquaintances but the real import is through group souls.

How can I put it over to you? In some ways it is simple and in others highly complex. You see there are always lots of different ways of looking at things. Patterns are important and what has been worked out in one life can mean a simpler, easier ride in the next but anything which was meant to be dealt with and was not simply comes round again. This is why it is foolish to commit suicide. In a particular life, you will take a certain vibration, quality or intention – bringing forth a virtue and strength in that virtue.

Take my own case, for example. As Albert, I needed to release pent up resentments and interior rage, brought over from an earlier time and my prime lesson was to develop patience. That was the life virtue but it wasn't the only thing – love was of paramount importance and seeking a channel in which to express that love. Moreover, there were gifts I'd developed in former times to be re-lived, re-discovered and carried a stage further. I had also lined up a life of challenge. In fact, I made it hard for myself. No plums on a plate – a difficult childhood and lack of financial means. There was no family pressure as such yet the lack of financial backing, emotional support etc. had an effect. I was deprived of my mother at an early age which caused a stunting of emotional growth. I did love; I loved you all very much but was in many respects an emotional cripple and couldn't express it at all easily. Because of having to rely on myself and stand on my own feet *(at an early age)*, I became self-reliant and self-protective. I always thought of myself first and others later. I was greedy materially in many respects – always saw that I had more than my fair share of grub and sufficient clothes. Your mother was the one who went without, to my eternal shame. As usual, it was a case of the vices of our virtues.

However, you don't see these things at eye level, only later when you come into the observational mode; then it's too late for the life that's been lived. It all goes into the record book and in time the opportunities to make a better show of it will be built into the pattern of the new life.

There were actually several Alberts. This is what I mean by the complications – and it's not going to be easy to explain to you – it is not about sub-personalities; all are equal but we bring over pieces from this one into that one and come up with a composite. There were several pathways for each Albert but because of fears, not taking risks, being lazy and taking the way of least resistance, I brought about a lack of identity, and the alternatives were not given a chance. I could have gone one of several different routes but it is unusual for any person to do this – we all usually end up as a composite. This is the main reason we are all so contradictory. Now, where does all this come from? Well, of course, the more lives we've lived, the more complex it is.

In my previous life, also as a singer, I had to manifest love. Often I was boorish; I was arrogant and rather care-free but I did have a love of music and people were subservient to that. I cared for my family but not enough. I tried to bend them to my will and to turn them into carbon copies of me. I had to learn that this isn't allowed. Yes, they were all musically talented – yes, they had to make their way in music – that was their chosen path, but I drove them with a whip and damn near knocked all the music out of them. I have much reparation to make on that score. Thus, I had a karmic debt to love when I came in as Albert; but as Albert, I strove to develop patience as the life lesson – this was, of course, linked with the last life and not something out of the blue. So, not just love which had been misappropriated, to be developed, but patience because I had not been prepared for their talents to unfold naturally but tried to drive them out with a 'big whip'.

I was a minstrel of various sorts in different lifetimes. I was in a monastery in the Middle Ages and loved the singing there *(Assisi)*. I also knew you in Salzburg (*16th century*) as I was one of your court musicians. I played the lute and sang. I also sang in church services.

As a 17th century soldier, I sang all the time. I gambled and played hard and was a roistering fellow. That of course, was a balance to the previous lives of monasticism and the ecclesiastical court. The soldier was in the outside world – the rough and tumble of everyday life – and I went over the top.

So, you see, I have only been dealing with my masculine incarnations so far but there is always a pattern. It is complicated when you see, in addition to the life you have lived, the other examples you could have lived, but how you've also dipped into each of them at some time and brought forth a composite. It is all very fascinating but the failures do rankle and it is hurtful to see the harm you've done and how you've hurt others. However, it's wonderful when you discover something you achieved; you've no idea how lovely that is – not only your own feelings but the feelings of those you helped which are amplified.

I don't think I can go into any more now, Barb, but it's given you something to think about. I've found it extremely hard to give you a correct mental picture which you could transcribe into words. I see it as strands of coloured light, weaving and interweaving, bringing forth frequencies which provide levels of understanding. I also see and hear as on a film. I am not always sure exactly what I am seeing at first, and it's almost like going into hypnotic regression to reach a level where I can wholly integrate and identify myself in those other lives. The beauty of it is that, as I let go of the dross and baser desires, my wholeness takes over and I am then able to correspond with my Higher Self who sends me messages and allows me to take into myself the knowledge of the intrinsic course and causes of a life.

I have not met my Higher Self face to face. That is still some way in the future. I have yet to hone myself into a wholeness to do so but I look forward avidly to the moment. I have to rise up many notches higher to be able to make that close contact but it will come and it is the most enlightening and fascinating work to concentrate on, developing this wholeness.

Some people re-incarnate more quickly in their haste to get on with it and so do not draw near enough to their Higher Selves. They are the ones who are usually pretty sceptical about spiritual matters because they are not sufficiently in touch with the Higher Self. However, if those to whom one has to repay debts are incarnating (*at the same time*) it is like running for a bus. One has to take the risk. I did not know your mum last time around *(19th century when he was a professional singer)* but I did in the soldier's lifetime. Again, I had to make amends but didn't make an awfully good go of it. I had cared for her quite a lot but let her down when I had to go away. She had a child, Hildegarde,[79] who I never met. In those days it was not so easy to keep in touch. The girl did quite well for herself and rose up in life to become a courtesan at the court at The Hague. It is all fascinating but more anon. We could go on forever but the power has been strong and we both need a rest.

Thank you, darling, for trying. The more you can find time to link with me, the stronger it will be and we'll be able to discuss all manner of things.

Some years later I discovered that my mother, though having been a lowly German woman in the 17th century was born at the end of the 18th century as Princess Charlotte of Prussia, who became the wife of Nicolas I of Russia, and as Tsarina, took the name Alexandra Feodorovna. The princess was a well-trained pianist and this accounts for my mother's natural pianistic ability as she only had two years of piano lessons as a child. Sometimes a previous skill is brought over from the past but not always. Reincarnation is all about balance and the blacksmith in one life may become an aristocrat in another one. The entity will change sex from time to time and it is quite possible that the psychological aspect of homosexuality is accounted for by these changes. For instance, if someone has experienced successive lives in a female body, it will

---

[79] Hildegarde reincarnated as his daughter, Mary, in Albert's 20th century life.

not be easy to adjust to a male body or vice versa. Our individuality is built up by the experiences gained in successive incarnations and remains the core of our being, but like an actor donning a costume, we assume a different personality with each incarnation in order to gain the widest experience and develop balance. I now hold the view that we have one life but play many different roles from age to age.

As the physics of earth are very different to those of a metaphysical realm, it is possible that even when a person has reincarnated, their previous selves are, as it were, in a library so can be telepathically contacted, even though the individuality has an aspect of itself living within a new personality on earth.

Later that day Dad tuned in again and gave more details of his previous lives.

I was already at court *(in Salzburg)* when you arrived *(as a male)*. I was then in my fifties and died five years later. I liked you, though many didn't, because you were hard and distant. However, you were fair, and your love of music was true. You were highly knowledgeable and well-trained, having been a canon (*a Jesuit*) of the Roman Catholic Church since your youth.

I was born again six years later by earth time. I wanted to try my hand in the outer world. Some of my former lives had been in quiet backwaters where I was able to work on the inner self and with music but I wanted the balance of the outer world so next time, I chose a much rougher life. It certainly toughened me up and I did enjoy it, but because for several lives I had had no experience of women, I went haywire.

Soon Dad told me that he was moving on to another level. This is what is known as the 'Second Death' which takes the person further away from the vibrations of earth, but he said that from there he would, at some point, reincarnate on earth. Through sharing his post mortem experiences, he had taught me a great deal and it is hoped that the book which he and others inspired will enable readers to realise that what we do on earth is important in the larger picture because life is eternal and does not end with the demise of the physical body and the links of love are for all time. However, for those who carry hatred in their hearts, or cannot forgive, chains continue to bind them from generation to generation; "the sins of the fathers to the seventh generation" as the Bible states.

Chapter Fifteen
The Dominance of Love

My cousin, Ralph, was sixteen years older than me and his wife Sheila was seventeen years older. I was very fond of them both and I enjoyed staying in their delightful home in Tynemouth, such as when I was on tour with Glyndebourne, singing at the Theatre Royal in Newcastle. They never showed their age but were full of fun and had a great social life as they were so popular.

Sheila was a gifted interior decorator who ran her own business and had a showroom in Newcastle while Ralph worked as a representative for the paper manufacturer, Wiggins Teape.

He had been in the RAF in India during the war and always smoked a pipe but it was a blow when Sheila rang shortly after my father died to say that Ralph had been diagnosed with lung cancer. At the time they were about to legally adopt Tim, a teenager from a local orphanage. Sheila knew that I was involved with healing and colour therapy and asked if I could help. She was ready to try anything but though Ralph humoured us, he was rather sceptical because he trusted in doctors, whereas I was a layman. However, I sent him colour therapy, healing and meditation cassettes and through my group absent healing was sent.

As he had to give up work, at least for a while, Sheila wanted to keep him busy because she was afraid that he would get bored but my guidance advised rest. To our delight, the tumour began to shrink; however, he developed fluid in his lungs which the doctors kept removing.

A few years later I read that Harry Edwards, a notable spiritual healer who had great success with cancer patients, said that this often happened en route to recovery. However, as far as the doctors were concerned, Ralph was an enigma. One day, Sheila dropped him off at the hospital for a check-up but had to go to see a client, so she was not there when he asked the doctor for a prognosis. Without prevarication, he told him that his case was terminal and there was nothing further to be done. Ralph believed so much in the wonders of science that he accepted this verdict as a death sentence and died the following week. Sheila was furious because she really believed that he was getting better and that with patience and therapy he would survive. However, Ralph's belief in the doctor's pronouncement was so strong, that he turned his face to the wall and died.

The following message came from our cousin, Greg, (the grandson of my mother's brother, John). He lived in Australia and was a talented young actor and singer but was killed in a motorcycle accident when he was eighteen. We had never met him but when I had a major operation in 1978, I became aware of a young man with horn-rimmed spectacles, who sat by my bed each afternoon while I was recovering. He was full of humour and made me laugh and was such a tonic that he enabled me to get back on my feet again. At the time, I thought he said his name was Ned. I had only seen a photo of Greg in make-up and costume for his role as Jesus in 'Jesus Christ, Super Star', but later my mother sent me a photo of him as himself and I realised that 'Ned' was Greg.

12th December 1987

Hello, old chum, great isn't it? Dandy Dinkum. Slowcoach, get a move on. Why aren't you writing as you usually do? Why sit and wait? We need the motive power of your arm moving then we can get going, get started, OK?

Guess who it is! You don't have anything to fear – we come to do no harm – just to make contact. It's comforting to be able to tune in and work with you. How about it? Just keep your pen on the paper and keep your head clear; don't try to formulate thoughts, they'll only distract. Just keep the pen moving that way we can keep going.

Now, you want to know how Ralph is, right? Well, he's OK and not half enjoying exploring the new realm. He isn't that keen yet to come into earth vibes; much as his wife would like him to. He's had enough for the time being and is enjoying his newfound freedom but don't tell her that – it would break her heart. In time he'll be able to link in on a fresh wavelength and she will understand more but at present, she's only aware on an earthly level. She doesn't really understand when you tell her about other dimensions. She has so much to learn. Sure she loved Ralph but she loves herself more. He was her purpose for living; now she has to stand on her own feet and live for herself. Believe me, she won't find it easy but she will find her strength. It is not easy for any of us but we all have to do it sometime or other

We've been watching for a while and see that she has drained you to a greater extent than you realise.[80] You have kept her sane, do you know that? Yes, she powered Ralph to keep calm and optimistic but she couldn't experience for him. He had to do that for himself and he has done so. Good on him. Never mind, and don't be despondent; she'll win through and win her colours. She's a great girl and well-liked.

Now, what about yourself? Where are you going – do you know? You feel you're sitting on your backside doing b… all, don't you? Well, let me tell you, you are and it's for a purpose. You've never been idle and never will be; you have an enquiring mind and a love of learning. Well, you've certainly learned a lot and there's more to come, so stand your ground and wait for it. You like being busy? OK, you'll be as busy as you please. This is the lull before the storm: boy, are you going to be kept moving! The stuff you've accumulated will all be kept up and used. More people than you think will open their hearts to you; this is what you've been trained for, and others like you. Few want to give themselves

---

[80] She was in Tynemouth and I was in Harrow, so the contact was tenuous.

as completely as you've done: there are always excuses but nothing you've done will be wasted. Interior doors will open and you'll be able to draw on things long forgotten. Experiences once dearly bought will become available to you again in this life. This isn't just for your own satisfaction but because it's necessary for others too. Have courage and step forward into the light. I'm not allowed to say too much; it has to open up step by step and you're not quite ready at this time. A lot is being given to you on inner planes when you sleep because deeper levels can be more easily accessed in sleep.

Don't worry, you're guarded and guided. Your acceptance of truth and your willingness to keep going without much to go on is appreciated. You've convinced and helped others even when your own strength was limited. There will come a day when the blinkers will be off and you will see and hear clearly into other realms, then you will know more fully.

At present, so much has to be taken on trust but this will change and much will be revealed to you so that you can reveal it to others. Those who are ready will be drawn to you. It is arranged in spheres beyond this one and is the reason for your present incarnation. There is to be a renewal of energies and a building up of potency in order for you to accomplish much that would tire even a younger person. Realise that this is not of yourself alone – you provide a physical package whereby greater strengths than yours can manifest, bringing peace and benefaction. Yours is not the way of the mystic or even the teacher in the accepted sense – it is a way of life in many guises, not just physical life.

An abundance of knowledge is being lavished on the earth plane and people have been planted in all walks of life in order to bring to the notice of the general public the real truths – the utmost realities. Mankind is asleep and must be gently awoken. There will be mayhem in many areas as this takes place; as the centuries of doubt and illusion fall away. Not all will be able to deal with such potent forces and will go haywire, developing mental illness and fanaticism in many cases. It is already happening in acts of mindless violence. These people are not fundamentally evil, just unready. However, they will be helped if the light can penetrate their darkness.

Your husband carries light and gives you insight and healing. He is a balancing, stabilising force and extremely important in your development. As long as you are manifest in the world, your husband will be with you. When the time comes to be evacuated to higher realms, you will transit together. You will find yourselves out of the body at the same moment and experience together, in perfect consciousness, the immensity and greatness of the life beyond.

Do not fear physical separation; it will not come as you envisage but will be of a greater magnitude than anything of which you can conceive with a physical brain.

Your son has his own path to take but his pattern is similar to yours. His life will be longer than yours so he will see a great deal of the twenty-first century. He is geared to be a very old man indeed 'ere he departs to another level. He will never lack a friend and will bring peace and plenty to many a soul in need.

You will notice an Antipodean flavour in the first part of this epistle because one of our numbers has experience in that part of the world in his last incarnation, and in using earth language, he easily falls into the old pattern. We are many in number. We watch and we guide. We prompt and we uphold individuals in times of weakness. We never sleep but are always on call in the interests of tried humanity. All is according to plan; you cannot do otherwise than fulfil your destiny.

The Law is great – go forth in peace and in love at all time; child of the time that is now.

23rd December 1987 at 3 pm

Ralph's apologies for having taken off like that. There was no time to say goodbye; no time to let Sheila know how much she'd always meant to him but the urge was too strong; it was like a great wind lifting him up and the light was too beautiful to resist.

There is no need to mourn – he is more alive now than he's ever been and has been exploring his new surroundings. He was not much interested in his funeral; it all seemed too trivial in contrast to what was going on in the sphere of light he had reached.

It was a bit like being hypnotised – he soon forgot earth conditions in relishing the feeling of space and expansion, which he found exhilarating beyond measure. Now he is becoming aware of what he has left behind and is desperately sorry for Sheila's loneliness and distress and tells her, "take heed of what Tim says – he has an old head on young shoulders and knows a thing or two."

Tim will not leave Sheila in the lurch but will strengthen and uphold her and there is an inrush of love each time she thinks of Ralph in a positive way, remembering the good times, as it makes him feel warm and responsive.

He is not yet able to control Barbara's vibes to write through her directly but must use her through a messenger, one who knows the ropes. There are three dogs with him, one is Susie. Mrs Previne has been to see him and he asks Sheila if she remembers her. She kept a corner shop; he also asks, "What about winkle pickers?" *(Exaggerated, narrow shoes, fashionable in the 1960s)*

Muff *(Ralph's mother)* sends her love and looks lovely; young, with flowing long hair down her back. *(When she was a girl, she was very proud of her long hair on which she could sit)*. Ted *(his father)* is just the same, chatting away with whoever will listen. He thanks Sheila for all she did for him and says he appreciated it even more once he went over and saw what a trial he'd been but Sheila never let on. He will do all he can to impress her thoughts with joy and optimism because she deserves the best.

Remember, it's only a period of waiting; there are no goodbyes, only au revoir and one day you will all meet up again, but in the meantime, you've got a lot to do, Sheila, and must use your time on earth well. There are so many hopeless souls around and you have the means to cheer them up. Try to take the long view and use the time you've been given constructively. It will stand you in good stead for later development.

Ralph was ready to go, as much as he loved Sheila and Tim; it was a strain for him to hold on. Finally, things had gone too far and he had to let go. Sheila can carry on for him; tell her that just talking to people and brightening them up is healing. It's great to be able to raise morale.

He's now steadying down a bit; at first, he was literally over the moon with it all, just like a kid on holiday. Now he's starting to see Sheila and Tim and is drawing near so that he can be with them in their Christmas celebrations. "Now, no being morbid," he says, "if you could see me, you'd think I was the one who is alive because I'm full of beans – well, bright, happy and knowing I can be with you as much as I want. Just run your thoughts to me – include me in your toasts – have a glass for me and remember, I'm with you – don't go shutting me out talking about me as a has been – remember, I'm as large as life and twice as natural."

"I've got quite a few people to see on this side, but at first I was drunk with delight and couldn't calm down enough to stay with them. I was legless and no mistake, only I didn't have a hangover.

"Now, remember to enjoy yourselves – no long faces – and I say again, don't think about me as 'dead', that I'm not, and my new body is much nicer than the old one ever was and does exactly what I want – although it often goes too fast for me and I whiz off into space then it takes me a while to balance and get back to where I began. I'm told in time I'll get used to this but I haven't got enough control yet.

"Anyway, Shiel – this is a time of living apart for a while – we'll have to link by 'telephone', Barbara being the apparatus – just imagine I've gone away on business, just as if the firm had sent me to live in Japan or somewhere outlandish like that; I may be out of sight but don't let me be out of mind.

"Muff and Ted send their love and want you to know they care for you as always and think of you as a real daughter. Please include me in your conversations; encourage people to refer to me, that way I can keep a firm link. It's sad when the 'dead' are forgotten or buttoned up.

"Life is what you make it and just because I'm not around doesn't mean you must live like a nun – get out and about and have a good time, just like we used to. You know how you love people and they take to you too, so none of this sitting about moping or I'll come and haunt you. Joking apart, look forward to the New Year, think of Tim and setting that little terror on his feet, and put your back into all the things you most enjoy doing. I'm sure all will be fine.

"Make 1988 a success as a single girl – and think of all we'll have to talk about when we really meet up again. In the meantime, take time to sit quietly with a cup of tea and link with me. Just talk to me in your head as you once did with words. Chat things over and I'll do my best to respond. Until then, you dear girl, be happy and love me still, as I do you, forever and forevermore – Gosh, look how poetic I'm getting now I'm on my way to the stars!

"I seem to be getting the hang of this – it's great. I'm going to be with you a lot more now I know how. We can still be Darby and Joan if we want to, what's a little thing like death to separate us?

"Keep your pecker up and give us a smile – that's my girl and thanks, Sheila, for being such a marvellous wife, nobody ever had a better one – I never wanted for anything, thanks to you.

"We'll be together on Christmas Day, don't worry. It's pretty important over here too. In fact, all the levels come together because the Christ ray links everything *(with no thought of creed)*. It's the celebration of the Cosmic Christ energy, not just on earth but throughout the universe.

"My special love to you, Shie, and to Varna and Tim and the others too, and thank them on my behalf. I love you all."

24th December 1987

Sheila's mother, known as Gyp, sent her a message via me. She said she was looking after Ralph. Sheila's parents had been on the stage and were considered rather exotic by Ralph's family. Gyp admitted that when Sheila first met Ralph she did not think him exciting enough for her daughter. She wanted Sheila to have someone to show her the world.

However, as she grew to know him better, she realised that Ralph was an ideal husband who gave Sheila the security and comfort she had missed in childhood. He had a quiet strength and Gyp accepted that Sheila desired a totally different way of life from her own. She was delighted that Sheila now had Tim and said she couldn't have a better friend than that boy.

Gyp revealed that the evening would be a time of gathering from their side and that the Watch Night Service would blend their auras together. At such times great power is generated and all would feel the emanations of relatives and friends on the 'other side'. She said that Ralph was being enfolded in their midst and their force and energy would help him to link with Sheila; enabling her to feel more love than she would have believed possible. A Cosmic link was being forged.

12th January, 1988 a.m

Settling down nicely now. Thanks for the prayers. Get Sheila to a Spiritualist meeting. Can't promise anything but will do my damnedest to come through. Depends on the medium, of course, but if she's good and there aren't too many others in the queue, I should stand a chance.

I know she appreciates the messages but I think it would make all the difference to her to know I was actually there. She's a great girl and her courage overwhelms me. I knew she'd miss me but never realised just how much, but still, she's trying to keep going and put on a brave face. It really does help me when she's able to stay more cheerful and remember all the good times. I can then draw very near and every time she thinks of me she draws me to her. If only she realised how near I am. Of course, it's difficult for her to believe this because she doesn't really understand how it can happen. But it's very simple; she thinks of me and there I am. I know what she's thinking – it's as if I can see inside her head. I draw into the lovely coloured field around her and feel warm and cosseted and wanted, just as I always did when folded in her arms. It's really even more beautiful now because we are able to completely blend.

I'm sorry Shie has gone down with the flu. It's only to be understood with all she's had to cope with. Her defences were really down so her body's making sure it gets a rest and recharges the batteries. She must take care of herself and not worry too much about Tim; he'll make out good. He's a great chap for coping. Anyway, they have made their decision and it seems OK to me. If they feel like changing their minds later that's OK too. Just see how things work out. Always ask for help and in one way or another it comes, but you do have to ask.

I know it's not easy but if Sheila could get to a meditation class or circle she might become more aware of me. Go into Newcastle. Look in the Yellow pages and see if any Spiritualist places are listed. You will feel drawn to one of them and will find some loving souls there. There will be more confirmation for you, Shie, if you're a stranger there.

Anyway, take youngster along if he'd like to go (I like the 'Dad' bit on the flowers – thanks!) You'll be drawn into this sort of thing more and more, you know. I'll do all I can to help. I couldn't stay to help at that end, so we'll be a partnership from this end. Give yourself a bit of time to come round and get well again. I think of you and watch you so much. I am with the dogs. Love you more than ever, Your Ralphie.

Chapter Sixteen
Guidance

12th January 1988

Although many people are unaware, we all have a guardian angel and 'inner' guides who are sometimes seen in clothes they wore when on earth. Everyone is potentially psychic and with regular meditation, the guides can become familiar to us.

In one of my own meditation sessions, I mentally asked to be told my true calling in life. A guide appeared with a tray on which were various tools. She gave me to understand that these were only symbols as the choice was mine. However, whatever I chose as my main focus in life, I would be assisted from an unseen region.

This is a message from the guide who appeared in the guise of a nun wearing a deep blue habit.

I'm so glad you are tuning in to me. There are many things I can do to help you and am only too delighted to do so. Thank you for thinking of me so kindly and trusting yourself to me. It has been a test of my patience to sit quietly by and watch you develop. Yes, you have other nun guides; (*I had sometimes been aware of a Sister of Mercy, with a huge winged white headdress, yet she was not the 'blue nun*). I am your permanent 'door-keeper'. It was I who entered with you at birth and will stay until you quit this plane.

I know you better than you know yourself and have often grieved with you over the frustrations (*of life)* but believe me, you have done well to keep on and aren't you glad that you did? You are enjoying your voice because you are mastering it and it is sounding lovely.

I find it exciting and really enjoy listening to you. I love your feeling for beauty and am very glad to be with you. It was a great thrill when, on the journey to Great Yarmouth, you saw me etherically. *I was on my way with colleagues to give concerts and we stopped at a restaurant for lunch. On a table nearby was a wine bottle with a picture of a blue nun on the label and though I don't drink, something drew my attention to it and I saw her very clearly in the room.*

As you will appreciate, it is one of the tasks of a 'door-keeper' to learn patience. Few people in earth bodies are able to observe and get to know their guides, although those who are sensitive sometimes feel the presence and atmosphere around a guide.

I just wanted you to know how pleased you have made me and how I look forward to assisting you in your work. Surely you can feel my delight? You have been in need at times and because of that you now have a more tender heart and can appreciate the sufferings and needs of others.

All is well and the light is bright around you.

Your 'Ancient One' is a more advanced soul than I am. He guides from a more advanced level than I and is concerned with your soul pattern. He has been with you many times and is conscious of your spiritual development. He is now able to vibrate at a faster speed because your vibrations have increased.

I asked to be with you because I had known you in a past age. I was drawn to music and realising that music would play a large part in your life, I wished to be with you.

I hope I have served you well. Through this opportunity to serve a soul living on earth, I have learned and developed with you. Thank you. Your loving Bernadette.

12th January 1988, 6.30 pm

Yes, you have the name right. It was my name in my last incarnation. You asked me to help with healing but I am not actually a healing guide. I am more limited than that as I am virtually your 'shadow' and my task is to stay with you at all times, repelling boarders but allowing those with noble purposes to draw near. I speak to you through your own mind; this is the channel I have to use to link with your consciousness. However, I can call on those more advanced than me and often have when you have needed help, both as a child and as an adult. I love you very dearly and am closely linked with you. I am in you and you in me. Thus I applied (*for healing*) for your lady – she is known. She can be helped but she is a stubborn character. Her ideas and attitudes are so rigid that it is difficult to get past them. However, there is a lovely soul there who has chosen a hard path. Life has not been easy but has been much enjoyed and small pleasures are appreciated, as much as far larger ones.

Keep her on your healing list and tune into her each day. Remember to say a prayer for her and she will be helped but it will be gradual for she has to be won over on a deeper level. There is much fear under the surface due to the severity of the upbringing and pressures of the dogma of her church.

However, she is lovely and deserves help. Keep sending her light. There is now a larger measure of help coming her way. Please get the music copied for her as soon as possible. This will be her salvation; having time to sit and quietly absorb these lovely vibrations. It will do her more good than any patent medicine.

Whenever I can be of assistance, just call – I am always within earshot. God bless you.

Chapter Seventeen
Ralph Returns

19th January 1988

Hello again, Shie, dear. Well, here we are once more. I gather it is Tuesday when Barbara makes herself available to write. You have a bit more to go on now and we'll see what crops up in the future but for now, we'll have to make do with Barbara. It's not ideal, I know, but better than nothing. She does her best and we're ungrateful not to acknowledge that. I wish I'd known a few more things before. I was so ignorant – well, aren't we all, or most of us, anyway.

I love it here but naturally, do miss you and look forward to being together again. Don't think of coming over for a while though, because you have that 'big lump' of a boy to get through college and into the way of working and that's going to keep you busy. Also, you'll grow by having to make your own decisions and stand on your own feet. We all have to, you know. I'm having to do it now. It's good to be a partnership but part of our lot is to develop our individuality, so I suppose we have to accept these separations for a while.

I'll let you know if there's anything you can do to help my development and don't think that's not possible because it is. We still help each other, even though no longer in the flesh. I can draw near to you and fill your energy field with good thoughts and love, and you help me by bearing up, being brave and sending your love to me. It's all reciprocal, you know.

Well, how do I occupy my time, you ask? First of all, we don't have time as you know it. There is no day or night – we all contribute our own light. Mine is fine, no worry; I live in a very light and colourful area. The trouble is I never developed my imagination, so am a bit dependent on what I can find here that's been created by others. I quite like the thought of learning more about mechanics, various mechanisms of different kinds. I can go back to old models; in fact to first models, like old engines, some of the first car engines as well as modern ones and what is to come in the future, such as cars running on gas, solar power and all that jazz. Sounds a bit daft to you now, I suppose, but there it is.

I'm still exploring and examining possibilities but as I didn't have a specific interest while on earth, I am open to ideas, but there is no rush to decide what I would like to specialise in. In the meantime, I look around and see what others are up to – if I don't get in their way, that is. I still like the odd drink in the pub and meeting and chatting to kindred souls and old pals. Do you know some of them have forgotten their old names; isn't it odd? Hope I don't but I've got you to remind me so that's OK.[81]

Barbara's getting tired; mustn't stay. Yes, just wanted to tell you there are some splendid buildings here and lovely parks and gardens. It's like ideal conditions on earth if that was possible. Don't worry; I'll keep in touch one way or another. Love you – Ralph.

21st January 1988

Hello there, Barb, dear Coz. Sorry if I seemed rude yesterday. Didn't mean to pass you by but was intent on talking to Shie and forgot the 'telephone'. We couldn't manage without your motive power, could we?

What I want to tell Shie has to do with the solicitor. Don't think too much about the pros and cons; just do what you want to do. If you try to consider everybody you'll get in a mess and end by pleasing nobody. Tim is the one you've to consider. The others all have partners to support them but this lad has to go it alone with us gone. Hopefully, you'll be around for a while to get him started but do try to keep it simple. Also, the more complicated it gets, the bigger the fee will be. There isn't a lot further to add. You know me; I couldn't be bothered with all the malarky of legal matters. I always tried to keep to brass tacks. There's no other way unless you've got a vast fortune to leave. Just make sure you're alright and have enough to manage on. See that Tim gets a good training in business studies. The artistic side will come along too but basically he needs to spot the sharks and those who will gobble him alive.

Now you've had your fingers burned over the two outstanding bills. Don't let it upset you but forewarned is forearmed. Just because you're honest yourself, you trust everybody else and as you see, they're not all like that. Them as 'as the money hangs on to it! So, in future, just get a nose for these things. Don't take on a job without some cash on the nail – like a deposit. After all, you don't carry a lot of spare cash. You're not one of the big boys and you need cash in hand to pay your own suppliers.

I'm only advising you because I see a bit further now. I was just as easily led as you by a plausible customer, but anyway, just be a bit more wary in future, it's sad to have to be this way but unfortunately, it's the way of the world. A pity but there it is. Anyway, I'll do whatever I can to help, however little it may be; even if it's just to let you know that I care and that I still want to be involved. Take care of yourselves and be well and happy. Ever your Ralph.

Just a postscript: You know the bonds we cashed in some time ago? Well, how about using that money for a bit of expansion? I know we wanted to hold onto it for a while but I think it should be working for itself. If you get that shop on the corner started, you can put somebody in to be on hand all the time, while you and Tim are flitting about. Anyway, have a think about it. It's a risk I know but that's what business is about. Poor Barbara is a bit puzzled about all this as

---

[81] Although pubs seem very earthly; in a mind created zone, any desire can be made manifest.

she doesn't have any background knowledge – it's hard for her and me, 'cold' as it were.

Never mind, you'll know what I mean and that's what counts. Get out and about more as you feel better and really let the business be something to write home about. You'll make a good couple, you with the flair and Tim with his eye for business. He won't be quite as daft as we are, nor so easily taken in.

If you want to go on trying for your money, do but I'd cut your losses and get on with the next round. Don't waste your energies. Just don't be caught again. Try to vet people for their creditworthiness before you take on a big job. You can't afford to absorb losses of that size. I suppose over the years we've been pretty lucky because we haven't lost out much. Yes, I think that's finished now – I'll let Barbara go; it was rather a long PS. Anyway, till next time. All love to you all.

PPS: Hold on to the fact that I'm with you – I don't have any alternative with you calling out to me all the time. You must think I'm some sort of oracle. Death doesn't make us any cleverer, you know. But joking apart, I'll always be there when you need me and it's a great comfort to know how much you care.

25th January 1988

During my morning meditation, I unexpectedly received a message from our Aunt Lou, Ralph's father and my mother's sister. She was eighteen years older than my mother and was like a second mother to us children. A factory worker for most of her life, she was involved in the production of munitions during WWII. She was immensely generous and always full of fun, so had many good friends. She lost her baby grandchild, her daughter and her husband all within eighteen months but bore her losses bravely. For the whole of her married life, she lived off Birchfield Road, Perry Barr, Birmingham, but in the late 1950s the area was redeveloped, and her house was demolished. The close community of neighbours was dispersed and, at the age of almost seventy, she was moved to a high rise flat at Kingstanding. Once more, she accepted her lot without complaint but she had always said she would die when she was seventy. We told her not to be morbid but four days after her seventieth birthday, while taking a nap after her Sunday lunch, she died peacefully in her armchair.

We were all devastated and I regret that I wasn't able to go to her funeral because I was at the Edinburgh Festival at the time. It often happened that when there was a death in the family I was either abroad or in another part of the country.

Hello, I don't think I was expected but I hope it's in order for me to write through you. You don't know how much I've wanted to make contact but I haven't been uppermost in your thoughts and why should I be? It's a long time since my passing and you are now almost old enough to be a grandmother yourself. I remember the little girl and teenager, then you went to London and I left the earth plane.

108

I was so thrilled when you remembered seeing me in a dream at your old flat (1964). Well, that was exciting because you saw clearly what I was wearing. I did my best to project the image of the dress I was found in, knowing it would have relevance.

When I told my mother about the dream and described the dress, she confirmed that it was the one Lou was wearing when her friend found her.

Yes, you remember a kindly disposed but not very well-educated woman – a manual worker with average intelligence. That was the personality through which I incarnated and it placed me where I was meant to be for the experiences I had come to undergo.

I am pleased that you remember me so kindly and call me a 'second mother' to you. Yes, I loved you children. I would have liked more of my own but it wasn't to be and I had a substitute family in 'our Darth's', as we called her.

She really has done a good job; don't be too hard on her. Your ideals are high but not everyone can live up to them. She has done her best by her own lights and that is better than indifference, even if it sometimes causes confusion regarding another's path.

I am finding this a slow method of contact but that can't be helped. I am struggling to relay this by slowing down my own vibrant force field. I think that is the only way I can convey to you my present stage of life.

Now, I am not about to reveal any secrets of the universe – they have to be worked for and earned. You will be helped by others than I as you journey towards further development, set in train by your own soul.

I am a releaser but I also strive to bring strength into the field of the one who suffers. Often it would be better if a hold on the body could be maintained, as this would cancel out much of the Karmic backlog to be rendered but if it is not to be, it has to be deferred to another time. This may sound all very distressing and is, seen only from the material view point but once in the fields of light, strength is engendered and the soul strengthened to try again.

Everything has to be earned and everything paid for; that is the law (*universal law*).

God bless you all – the work proceeds; let the light shine forth at all time, for your intimate family, as well as your larger one. Louie, that was.

25th January 1988 (evening)
Ralph again:
Dear Shie,

I know you're in need of guidance and are going to ask for some tonight. Well, I'm already abreast of what's happening. You can't keep me out of things and being dead doesn't stop me being family and having my say!

Now, we're dealing with Tim's life and prospects and although he has to make his own decisions, it really strikes me as a bit 'pie in the sky' this boat lark.

First of all, that's the sort of job for a lad with no other prospects. OK, so it makes a nice working holiday and it's tempting to think of the sun but remember he'd be working in foreign parts, knowing nobody other than those on board the ship and not knowing the languages of the places visited. Also, in port there's still ship's work to be done. It won't be all beer and skittles. I'm not trying to be a killjoy but it has to be thought about. What if he's not happy and miles from home? What then?

Well, the way I see things, and you did want my opinion, is that it may not seem so glamorous but the laying of foundations now will pay off later – the education and the family business – there is no limit to what can be built up if Tim has the will and with you and your experience behind him.

As I said, the decision has to be his, but if the business does well and there's no reason to doubt it, then he'll be able to afford his own foreign holidays and not as somebody's lackey on a boat.

It's late and Barbara's had a very busy day, concentrating fully and now pretty ready to drop, so I'll let her go.

I'll keep in touch, don't worry and hope this will help. I know it's the thing uppermost in your minds and later we'll discuss other things. Goodnight you dear darlings, I love you, Ralph.

Sheila lived in Tynemouth, north of Newcastle and I lived in Harrow, a borough in north-west London. At that time we did not have access to mobile phones or email and long distance telephone calls were expensive. Ralph's communications would be typed by me and sent by post to Sheila. I was simply a go-between and did not know what questions Sheila was putting telepathically to Ralph, or that she was constantly calling on him, just as though he was simply in another country rather than a different dimension.

2nd February 1988
Dear Shie,

I know you're hoping to hear from me at this time. Can't take too long as there is a queue for Barbara's pen.

Well, you're getting by, I see. I know your distress at times but it's only natural; don't be despondent, it's early days yet and we miss each other. I've got so many things to tell you. There are good times coming up. You may find it hard to believe but really in a few months, the heaviest part of your grief will be over.

Much of this comes because you are not used to doing things on your own. We've always been able to discuss things together and combine ideas. Well, now you've got to learn to trust your own judgement unaided – also you've got to help Tim set himself up. You've always been a tower of strength to me; well, imagine it is still so because truly it helps me to have you link with me from earth. It's lovely to know people still remember and miss me but really if they only knew how close in thought I can be, they'd be staggered. Anyway, keep your cool about all the sorting out. This is inevitable after a death – there seems so much paperwork and tidying up to do as well as all the official things.

Well, this time next year you'll have all that behind you. Just do one thing at a time. There are always people to turn to. Get onto the firm (*his firm*) regarding BUPA and get that settled first. It will take a weight off your mind; then sort out things with the tax office. The pensions business will sort itself out and you will get your book back. They always take a longish time 'cos they're usually so short-staffed. Anyway, make full use of the solicitor; that's what he's being paid for. You'll see that when everything is sorted out you'll be better off than you think.

Make sure that the accountant is claiming all he can with regard to home and workplace being one. I think we haven't claimed enough in the past.

I see so many paths opening up for you and you are going to meet people who are not just clients. You will be drawn to places and meet quite different sorts of people to those we've usually been associated with. You're going to become quite popular as a sort of 'agony aunt'. People will open their hearts to you and you'll be able to help them.

I know you will find this difficult to imagine because you feel it's quite enough coping with your own lot at present, let alone anybody else's but in time, as you are able to master and overcome your own grief and problems, you'll find yourself capable of helping others worse off than yourself.

You know, whatever you say and think, there always had to be a parting. If I hadn't gone first, I'd have had to go through what you're experiencing and remember, we are still conscious on the 'other side'. I miss you too but I'm luckier than you because I can draw near and see you. Mind you it's not easy when I'm right beside you and you can't see me. It is frustrating but sometimes, and I feel really chuffed then, I can get you to feel my presence and that's lovely. I feel so sorry for you when you cry and can't feel my arms around you, comforting you and telling you really, all's well and you haven't anything to despair about, because I'm really there beside you. I know every time you're thinking about me; it's like somebody pulling on a bell rope and I'm aware and know who it is.

Now, I've taken up more than my time but I must say I'm glad you've taken steps to start developing – eventually, we'll have our own communications system but just hasten slowly; it's never easy but you can do it, so can Tim and it will really enhance your lives, then you can tell others and that's how it spreads.

Just keep up the good work and know I still care and always will. That has to be all for now. With all love, Ralphie (what a daft name). Never mind, I'll hang on to it!!

111

Chapter Eighteen
Airmen

Early one morning, in 1985, I was meditating before breakfast when I became aware of a seascape on my inner screen. My eyes followed the coastline as though I was watching a film then the coastal scene morphed into an airfield which I guessed was in England. At first, I saw planes from WWII then they became overlaid with planes up to the present day, as though they were on different layers of transparencies as a graphic designer or architect might use. Although these planes belonged to different decades they all occupied the same space. It was fascinating but I had no idea why I was observing such a scene. As I gazed, the picture became less distinct and I began to sense a presence on the right-hand side of my chair; I slowly turned my head and saw, to my amazement, the life size form of a man wearing WWII flying kit. He was actually in the room with me, not on my inner screen; while behind him, though slightly less clear, were three other figures in flying kit.

The first man asked me if I could help them. I did not know what he meant, then I realised that they were 'lost'. I had heard about Spirit Rescue but had no experience of it. However, at that time, I was quite aware of two inner 'teachers' who were training me, so I called on one of them. Immediately, I saw him clearly on my inner screen and mentally asked him to help the men. Suddenly the screen went blank, like a TV set being turned off and the men were no longer in my room.

As with many such experiences, although they appear very real, one always wonders if it is imagination. However, I could never conjure up such things for myself; they always happened of their own volition.

About three months later, I was browsing in the library of the College of Psychic Studies when a woman approached me. I did not know her but she introduced herself as a CPS lecturer and asked me if I was aware of the young airman who was standing beside me. She said he was in uniform and she could see wings on his jacket. Ralph was still on earth then and though he had been in the RAF, the contact could not be him. Although my meeting with the airmen had been a profound experience; strangely, I had totally forgotten about it. She then reminded me of the young airmen I had recently helped. Suddenly, it all came back and she said they had been trying to thank me ever since because as I sent out a call to my 'teacher', he appeared and projected a shaft of light that showed them where they had been all the time but hadn't realised. As they were in a timeless zone, they had been going back and forth to their airfield but no one took any notice of them. Finally, they realised that the war was over and they were adrift. They looked around for help and saw my light as I was meditating. Now they wanted to thank me but they said they had found it difficult because I was always so busy. After this, I became aware of them, particularly the skipper, tuning in from time to time, and the following is the only written example I have. There was a crew of seven originally so after they were killed, three of them must have found their way to where they were meant to be.

4th February 1988

Sorry if I disrupted things last night. I didn't intend to, as you might guess. I was as surprised as you, being aware of me (*It was during an exercise in sand reading that I was leading at the local further education college*). Fancy me making such an impression just because you had your hands in sand. *Sand contains crystalline particles that aid contact.*

I often call by to see how you're getting along but you don't notice me; why should you, you always have so much on your mind; it's a wonder you are able to register as many things as you do.

I've always wanted to say a personal 'thank you' and so have Peter and Bill. You have been aware of Peter more than a couple of times. He always appears in his flying kit and I in my uniform, just so you can tell us apart. I don't think Bill and Geoff's vibes register as clearly with you as Peter's, and mine really got to you last night.

Well, it was good when that medium was able to tell you I was trying to make contact. My goodness, you've got a lively mind; it's like waiting to dive into a pool crowded with people on a bank holiday. Never mind, here we are. Who would believe such things? Not the average chap in the street. Well, theirs is the loss. Mind you, I can't criticise; that's how I was, and the others. Nobody had ever told us of such things and we'd never enquired. That's how we found ourselves in such a mess.

We were on a sortie to Germany – Frankfurt (1944) to be precise. We dropped our packet then turned for home. We seem to have been shot up a bit and the kite was not doing all she should. Anyway, we made it to the coast, literally on a wing and a prayer, but once over the sea, we considerably lost height. We were too low to bail out and the rest is history. We certainly knew something was wrong but didn't know what. It seemed we were in a blackout for a while – then we could see each other. We kept together – Geoff had hurt his leg; he was a rear gunner. I was skipper. Anyhow, Geoff's leg seemed to be OK. We wandered around for a while and then found another plane. *Their desire must have created an etheric one.* We carried on our duties – going back to the airfield but nobody took any notice. We didn't see any of the others in our condition; that's the strange part. Well, so it went on, we kept flying and gradually realised things were changing in Germany. We didn't have any bombs to drop – not that any of us wanted to have. We saw that things were changing as the rubble cleared. We knew we needed help but didn't know how to get it, and then, seemingly by chance, we spotted your light. You've no idea how lovely you look when meditating. No flannel – we didn't see your physical form only this attractive light glowing with colours. Anyway, as we drew near we became aware of the form in the light. You were like a signpost for us. We managed to make contact – I realise now you weren't aware of me at all, only William, we call him that to keep him in order; and Peter.

Well, thanks to you we were rescued. So many of our old chums turned up; as well as relatives and friends. Many had had quite long lives, whereas ours had been very short. We were all early 20s, Geoff only 19.

Your guide was a really good sort and explained things to us. We found ourselves in a garden and that's where we met some of the others. Then we had a good, long sleep. When we woke up, it was as if we'd always lived there. I shall be going on soon and I wanted to contact you before going, to let you know we care and always will. You've linked with us for all time, whether you realise it or not. Our lot was really horrible and you and your guide saved us. I don't know why we weren't picked up earlier. Anyway, now we're going away to start training so we can help others. There's going to be a lot coming over in the next few years and we're being prepared to be ready for them. We're told not to say too much as earth people get very worried and frightened. Anyhow, you are aware of quite a lot of these things even if you don't know the details. There will be happenings on a large scale so many people are being prepared to cope with the emergencies on your side and ours. Don't think we'll lose touch but I'm going up a notch which might make it that much more difficult to get this sort of contact. I loved flying; it was my life or would have been if I'd made it. Well, there is a new world and life awaiting me. We're all going to have it a bit rough – on your side and ours until we get over the hump. Keep chipper and your pecker up. It won't be too bad, but you'll all need to keep your heads down to avoid the flack. We all love you. Peter, Bill, Geoff and Sandy.

During the war, air Chief Marshall, Lord Hugh Dowding, who ran the Battle of Britain from Bentley Priory in Stanmore, was involved, through a medium, with the rescue of young airmen who had been shot down and jolted out of their physical bodies. Many of them were thoroughly confused and needed help to guide them to their rightful place. However, there was such little understanding of the spiritual world that many people thought Dowding 'not quite the thing' which damaged his career.

It seems that Sandy and others had been warned about such things as the Falkland's War; the Balkan crisis; two Gulf wars; Afghanistan, now Syria and Ukraine, as well as conflicts in Africa, not to mention worldwide terrorism and natural catastrophes, such as wide-spread floods, hurricanes, tsunamis, volcanoes and earthquakes; as well as the global financial meltdown and international disputes. Earth must certainly be keeping the denizens of the unseen dimensions very busy with the thousands of souls who are being sent over in large numbers.

Chapter Nineteen
More Contacts

The following message is an answer to a request for healing for a woman in her late sixties and was received on 7th June 1985. Although it is specific to that person, it could apply to anyone regarding possible causes of ill health, though it is also profound teaching regarding reincarnation and the necessity of balance from one life to another.

The subject wasted money in a previous life. In this life, she has learned to 'balance her books'. What appears to be limitations are in reality, opportunities.

She is learning to overcome her negativity and develop strength and fortitude. She is also learning not to force others from their patterns, difficult though she finds this because she always feels that she knows best and has foresight. However, she cannot remove the burdens of others; only lighten them. To provide a sweet, loving environment with calm vibrations is of more value. Practical help is useful but does not provide every answer; each must travel his own path in his own way.

Too much dominance causes others to lose their way. They have their own lessons to learn. If you always do a child's homework for him, he will fail his exams.

Resentment is a frequent cause of ill health. There needs to be a 'letting go' of old injustices and injuries because they inflict terrible suffering upon the body.

If a negative thought is tenaciously held, a festering occurs in the etheric body which produces the kind of illness which the medical profession finds difficult to cure. The physical body is the last resort; the mind and emotional body originate the disease.

When you do not treat a wound, it will fester and cause pain, spreading to other areas. This is how negative thought affects the physical organism.

Be content to provide warmth and loving comfort in the home where troubles can be overcome by sharing. Be not so proud. Forget your injuries – let the past go. If you refuse to forgive and forget those who have harmed you, you will harm yourself more. Resentment is a killer! It is your ego which hinders you. Be truly loving and kind; think not of your own feelings. Remember, if your enemy strikes you, turn the other cheek so that he may strike that too, but it is he who will suffer for it, not you.

Live only in love and faith. Know that you have protection and love at all time. Do not distance yourself from it by resentment and anger. You do valuable work and are loved for it. Your biggest stumbling block is love of self. This may seem a contradiction because you have a sacrificial nature and can be truly unselfish but you are also proud. You have wielded power; you have known position and a humble place does not sit well with you. However, you have achieved more in this present lifetime than you can know. Your path is set to the stars.

In future times when you have left this earth behind, you will look back on this incarnation as having been of great value. What seems important on the earth plane loses significance when you get beyond it. On earth, a humble life seems of little relevance, yet it is the stuff of soul substance. Many an important man becomes a pauper in the soul world. Difficult as it is for you to grasp, your soul knew of its necessities before it came to earth this round and it chose that which would be of most value to it. You have walked this difficult path well but there is still much which you could improve and which will give you greater satisfaction when you reach your next abode and look back over this life.

Be content; do not always desire the prime position: be happy to BE! Do not always strive to be the centre of attention or feel that you are failing if this is not so. Often the one who sits quietly in a corner attracts others to him; just as the one who insists on being on centre stage can repel. It is a point for you to consider.

This is not criticism but is for love of you and to save you unnecessary suffering. The merest trivialities assume vast proportion, causing turmoil all around you. Be gentle of speech and cultivate quietness. Rest in your thoughts; you live too much in the past. Live for the day in hope and gratitude. Your task is not yet done. Let your latter years be of tranquillity. What you cannot change, do not resent. You cannot live the lives of others. The right path is an exceedingly narrow one. Balance is needed as in a complex watch mechanism and your very strengths, if taken to excess can cause trouble.

You cannot live the life of another; provide love and comfort for their souls but let them go their own ways. It is your prime lesson at this time. You are a dear and loving soul and have had many buffetings on your journey. When you are able to see and understand many lives, the pattern will become plain to you and you will be amazed at the progress you have made in your present life.

Cultivate being a better listener and do not always desire the prominent part of the conversation. Be less concerned with your own activities. Think not of always providing money as the answer to problems. There are other ways.

To listen quietly and lovingly to the trials of others – providing a shoulder on which to lean and promoting a cheerful, optimistic outlook, will serve them more than all the gems of the universe. You will become ever more magnetic, like the sun, drawing all to you to bask in the warmth and love of your being. Let your heart sing and forget the heavy earth conditions. Lift up your heart to your home which is in Heaven, where dwells your Higher Self. Your personality is only the merest spark from that great soul.

The 9th of February 1988

On the above date, I received two communications; the first was from my German teacher at the Guildhall School of Music and Drama in London, Hilde Auerbach. She was a very cultured woman; a good pianist, with a deep love of poetry. She came from a wealthy Jewish family, and though she and her husband almost left it too late, they escaped to England in 1938. Due to immigration restrictions, she was only allowed to work as a domestic but after the war, she became a valued member of staff at Guildhall.

She was devoted to her students, who included the tenor Anthony Rolfe Johnson and my great friend, the composer, Charles Robin Broad, and they continued to consult her long after they graduated from Guildhall, as I did myself.

Hello Barbara,

How delightful to have this opportunity, at last, to thank you for all the help you have given me. I was so relieved and pleased when your prayers started to reach me shortly after I 'landed', as it were. They gave me so much comfort. I have been reunited with my dear brother and the little cat – yes, our worst fears were realised – the wretched woman had had the animal destroyed but we are now together again, dear Neville and I; never more to be parted. I loved that animal so much; it was a deep sorrow to me and to Mary[82] when he disappeared. Do please let Mary know that I am alright and that I now bow to her better knowledge. She was right and I wrong. Oh, yes, we certainly continue. Not for a moment did I lose consciousness. I was able to take it all in and to remember those who came to meet me. It was the highlight of my life – dying.

Such a great surge of love met me – I was bowled over by it. I did not realise how much I mattered to those I'd known and loved. No, there are no more separations and when Mary arrives here, that will make all perfect.

I was, strangely enough, not so surprised to find that I was still a living, breathing being. I had always believed I'd be puffed out like a candle; yet here I was, as large as life and twice as beautiful. I glowed. I could see my arms and limbs and they literally sparkled. From being old and decrepit, I was so light and full of life and joy. There were animals all around me and I felt I knew them all. They were not all domesticated animals, either, but some quite rare varieties; the sort seen in zoos or in natural habitat.

Well, I have settled down with many of them, so you could say I now have my own zoo, though there are no cages or bars and all my dear ones get on so well together. It is pure joy to be with such contented, unsophisticated and loving creatures.

Whenever you need help with your work; whenever you have to learn some German songs; call on me. I will help you. We will do good work together – think of all the wonderful Lieder.

---

[82] Mary was a nurse with whom she shared a house after her divorce.

I am told that I have to go now; I must not overstay my welcome. I did so much want to make contact and to let you know how you helped at our last meeting. You did not think so, nor did I, at the time; but you held up the veil for me when the time came and I knew. What more can I say except to send you heartfelt love and thanks. Hilde Auerbach.

Before I won my place at Guildhall, I was a member of the Theatre Society in Birmingham. It was a good amateur organisation with some professional stiffening with whom I played my first role on stage; Celia in 'Iolanthe' by Gilbert and Sullivan. There was a delightful woman in the wardrobe department whom we called Dr Elizabeth, as she was a GP. I never knew her surname. After I went to London, I heard that she had committed suicide. As she was always so cheerful, this was hard to believe. However, as is my wont when people die, I prayed for her for many years. However, I was very surprised when almost thirty years later, I received the following message.

Dear Barbara, You never expected to hear from me, I'm sure. Let me tell you I've wanted to contact you but didn't know how. Well, here I am. I can hardly believe it. Your nun (*my 'doorkeeper'*) is such a dear soul, so loving and kind. I am very pleased to be allowed to make this contact.

I feel I've 'come home' now; you know, of course, of the silly thing I did all those years ago. Now it seems so stupid and I cannot imagine how it came about. I suppose I was worn down with work. I had no one to love. I would so much have liked to have my own partner but I had to watch others pairing off and me the odd one out.

Well, one day, it all just seemed too much. One has to be very emotionally strong to be a doctor. When you see so many ill people and such depressive states, it rubs off. If your own emotional life is healthy you withstand it; well, mine wasn't. I had an elderly mother who was a trial and a brother who was married and that's it. He got away scot free and I was left to carry the can. Pa had died some time ago, so muggins copped the lot.

Now, I'm not belly-aching, just giving you the score. You see, I knew as soon as I'd done it what a fool I was to throw away my life when I had so much going for me. Yes, it really looked like that as soon as I'd drawn away. I was shown the life I should have lived. I would have eventually married a widower with grownup children; a loving and kind soul. My mother was due to die two years later and I would have been free. We'd never got on and didn't have the first thing in common. She'd always preferred my brother. Well, there I was, having thrown my life away; in even more despair than I'd been on earth. I had opted for a life of service to the community, qualifying as a doctor when it was not particularly easy for a girl. I'd achieved something fine and thrown it away.

Now I'd also upset the balance for the man I was due to meet later in life with whom I would have spent old age. His life was empty as there was no remarriage and no partner to care for him to the last.

118

I was in hell – literally. All was dark and grim as I tossed around in my own mind. I just couldn't forgive myself. I called myself all the names I could lay hold of, the stupid cow that I was. Your prayers, and those of others who cared, took me by surprise. After all, you and I were barely acquainted. You'll never know just how much light those prayers represented. I wasn't cast off; somebody cared enough to keep those prayers going.

Little by little, I began to take notice. I saw a guiding light and I followed it; that way I made contact with my own soul. It was disappointed at what I had done but so loving and kind and considerate to me, it filled me with its love for its creature, and I began to feel human again. I was loved after all. If only we were aware on earth of all that we can know afterwards when we see the results of our life – of the love we give to others and how they care for us. It doesn't have to be personalised as in a love affair, or with a particular partner; love is everywhere in everything.

My patients loved and needed me and I deserted them. But in time I came to forgive myself as my soul forgave me.

I have come to tell you that I am being reborn. The old Elizabeth is going into abeyance. I am to receive a new personality and body. Again, I shall be a doctor but this time as a man, as that way I shall have more command.

Although women are now more accepted, they still do not wield as much authority as men, so I've opted to be masculine.

I haven't got very far in 'after death' planes. Due to the action I took, I've stayed close to earth conditions and have now been given the opportunity to incarnate once more. I know it will be a hard life but I've acquired strength in the interim and now I feel I shall have a stronger link with my soul than I previously did.

Always do your best within reason, to persuade others that suicide is never the easy way out – always better to stay put and keep on keeping on, as they say.

Well, there's certainly a good deal of sickness in mind and body on earth. Also, there is a need for doctors who are real healers not just technicians. I am coming into a family of physicians, so I should have a head start. Wish me luck and keep praying for me. Elizabeth.
Saturday, 5th March 1988

Sheila and Tim were staying with me, Chris and Giles in Harrow, and in the evening, we chatted about Ralph and wondered if he would 'tune in' with me. The following is what emerged.

Of course, I'm here – how could you doubt it – do you think I'd miss up an opportunity like this? I've worked to get you all together again. I'm like 'cock of the walk' to think this is possible. Albert is here too; we are overjoyed to get the chance to speak to you all. Good old Chris; (*he had been keen for the rest of us to stop chattering and sit quietly*) we thought you'd never get going; such a lot of chin-wag. Never mind, as long as you're enjoying yourselves. We know we're never far from your thoughts.

Darling Sheila, You break my heart with your grief. I knew you would miss me terribly and that I was dear to you but I little thought just how dear and what a truly devoted wife you are. You are a good mother to Tim too, even though you chastise yourself for being miserable. Anyway, greetings, old chap, and thanks for all you're doing for Shie – I knew you wouldn't let her down.

Well, Sheila, your every thought reaches me and I get quite drenched by your tears – so let's have a bit more sunshine, old girl – OK? Don't act too hastily because at present you're not yourself and you will regret acting without proper thought and preparation. Just take each day at a time and gradually things will make sense. You've taken a long time to get your experience and expertise with the business – don't throw it away. You give a wonderful service, more than you realise; not just in a material sense, but in the love you deposit in the places where you work. You're not aware of this aspect but it's very real. You will forego this aspect if you allow self-pity to take over, or lose your interest in the work. What you do with and through love, that is what is so valuable.

You will find it hard to understand what I am going to tell you but in time it will make sense and as you have the desire, you will be given the opportunity to learn and discover things of which you are totally unaware. This way you will begin to realise and understand more of my way of life. The only barriers are the ones we put up for ourselves. There really is no separation. If only I could get this over to you but you cannot yet see things from where I stand. At present, I am immediately behind you. I see you all so clearly but it is as if I stand behind a plate glass window. I am looking out but you can't look in. I am without a physical body so I cannot relate to you on your own level yet I am not a wisp of light or phantom. On my own level, I do have a body and it's solid but it's a nicer body than the old one, though it looks very much like it; only I'm fairer. I think you'd like me if you could see me. I am trying very hard to link while you sleep then help you to remember and retain the information.

Albert is here too and sends you all his best wishes. He is so pleased Barbara is getting his letters together. It will help him to have others read them and he is not annoyed that he may appear in a less than pleasant light. It is all part of the new knowledge we have of reality and of the necessity to help others so that they learn to help themselves.

The 'juice' is running low and we have to withdraw from Barbara as we stand in danger of blowing her fuse. A little at a time but she too will grow stronger and will be able to take more of the 'fluence'. We love you all so much; even more than we did on earth because we see so much more now and understand in all sorts of ways that wouldn't have been possible before.

I sit with you both (*Sheila and Tim*) so often and join you at night. Get Barbara to show you the pictures she has in a Dutch book. (*Illustrating energy fields around humans*). That may give you a little understanding of how I am able to draw near to you. In time, you will be more aware of me but it will take an effort on your part; a certain discipline, but won't it be worth it? Gradually you will learn how these things manifest – there is no need to fear – I am not a ghost but a state of mind – and this is how we link – mind to mind, as I am doing at the moment with Barbara. Everybody could learn to do what she's doing but few will give the time and patience required to learning.

You both have gifts of which you are presently unaware but all the possibilities are there. Good luck to you. I love you so much, don't forget that. Stop thrashing yourself for any so-called shortcomings. You did all you could for me and I'll always be grateful for such love and tenderness. The decision had already been taken on a higher level – nothing you did could have changed that. You were and are a perfect wife. I've never had any complaints, so please, let's see again the fun-loving Sheila I fell in love with, all those years ago and who I love more than myself. God bless you, Sweetheart.

I'll be back as soon as Barbara can cope with me but don't worry, please. Take life as it comes and just trust that all will be alright. You will find yourself with lots to do in the future. I'm tied in with the work which is to come – it's to do with helping people as Barbara does and I shall be your 'control' and contact. We're a great partnership and it will continue – we're just going into the second round.

All love, hugs, kisses, etc to you all, Tim, Varna and the children (*young Italian friends from way back*). See you soon, your own Ralph (ie!!)

7th March, 1988 10.30 is

Thanks a million, Barbara, knew you wouldn't let me down. Sheila is waiting for a personal note from me. She is developing a new attitude of mind; thanks to you and all you've done for us. You're the best 'telephone' a chap could have.

What a lovely weekend it was – my Sheila was really two different people – one like a poor little old lady (never thought I'd see the day) – the other (on Sunday) was the one who will never age; so vital and full of gaiety and humour.

The more cheerful she is the closer I can come. I was at my closest this weekend and I never left her side. She is not yet sensitive enough to feel my presence but I'm there, nevertheless.

I can be in several places at once and it takes a bit of getting used to; quite a different experience to anything known on earth. Just because I am with Sheila doesn't mean I can't be anywhere else.

Yes, I've had great fun riding trams and trains. I've been a small boy again – eating toffee apples and having a whale of a time – no school – just treats. Great. Wait till you all come over, boy, will I show you a good time – you ain't seen nuffing yet. *He is referring to the etheric double of the Beamish Museum which was one of his favourite places when he was on earth.*

Well, you had a nice time on Sunday evening, didn't you? A bit low key and quiet but you all relaxed and enjoyed yourselves. It did my heart good to see Sheila looking so lovely and to hear her laugh again as in the old days.

Please, darling Sheila – dress up again for my sake. You don't seem to realise, I see you quite clearly and don't fancy being married to an old frump. So, throw away your wretched 'uniforms' and pretty up again.

What about that lovely emerald green dress – that's an eye catcher, get it out again – wear lots of makeup and jewellery and knock 'em for six. You're worth dressing up; you're just great to me; always were and always will be.

Tim's getting along with the good life too – I can see him becoming quite the connoisseur, given half a chance. You two are really going to take off you know and I'm looking forward to coming with you.

Please hang on to the old homestead. It's easy for me to 'wing' in there – might not find it so easy in a strange place. Of course, I can 'wing' in with you but a place that has my imprint so strongly is the easiest.

Since linking you and Barbara together at the weekend, I've found it easier to 'swan' in here too *(the house in Harrow)*. Of course, my vibes are here as well but not as strongly because I only visited a few times.

The flat is a credit to all concerned but most of all to you Shie, because your mind conceived it first of all and made it come to life. *Sheila had decorated a flat in Park Crescent, Regent's Park on behalf of clients.*

You'll have a marvellous time here; you'll be amazed at all the things you'll be able to create and the colours will blow your mind. We have colours here you've never dreamt of on earth. You'll be very popular too because you've developed your mind in that way and will be able to build things for those less talented then teach them how to devise creations for themselves. Some people are quite lost because on earth they've given no time to developing the imagination or artistic aspects.

Well, my dearest loves, I have to let Barbara get to her daily duties. I felt so excited at being able to get so close, I just had to write. I'm upsetting her time-table but she's a good soul and tries to comply!

Oh, I hear you asking; how I can be on my own level and with each of you at the same time; I can also be any place on earth for which I feel a curiosity. As I said, all this is possible and very common at my level. I suppose I just sort of 'tune in' and there I am; just as I'm tuning in with Barbara now. Try to find time to read – Barbara will recommend books, I'm sure, and it will help you as you begin to understand more. But in the meantime – just know, lock it right in your heart, that I'm with you – you haven't lost me – will never lose me (just try) and that I shall go wherever you go; I'm not just with you at home but everywhere. The very Cosmos isn't wide enough to keep us apart. You are me and I am you – how could we be parted? Gradually, you will know – don't let anybody, however close they may be to you, try to dissuade you. You know in your heart and have always known that we are one. Just keep praying for knowledge and wisdom to accept, as Barbara is learning to accept this irrefutable truth.

She is learning all the time and is becoming more expanded as fresh information reaches her. She is a continual searcher after truth. I would trust her with my all and so can you. She will never lead you astray but she too has known doubt, yet as she experiences more and more and knows, not just believes, so she is able to triumph over doubt.

People are well-meaning but stupid; if they have no knowledge or experience of such things, how can they presume to judge or to advise? Be strong in your heart and your own knowledge. I will do all I can to give you proof but some people won't believe, even if it is under their noses. Some are afraid to believe; others just don't care; don't think it concerns them – they're too tied up in everyday matters but no one escapes it. One day they will have to know and then they'll wish they'd taken more notice. Just keep your thoughts to yourself, unless you feel someone is ready and would benefit by them. As long as we know, it doesn't matter what anybody else thinks. If they think you've gone a bit peculiar – let them. Just smile and plod on; we'll have the last laugh.

Now, I really must release Barbara. I won't even say cheerio because I'm not going anywhere – that is, only where you go. Get that business on its feet – get off your bum and do a good day's work. I can't have a shirker for a wife, and go easy on the booze – you'll coddle your colour sense!

All love to you, dearest; and all the gang. I send my best to Percy Park (*his Rugby Club*) and all the loafers there. Your very own, Ralph(ie!!)

15th March 1988

Shie, dear, you've done my heart good the way you've perked up. Don't let any silly things spoil your new found optimism and trust. It's lovely to see and does make things easier for me. I'm so glad you and Tim see eye-to-eye and are getting on so well.

Glad to see you looking smart again too, that's my girl; give 'em a run for their money – you're only young once. Well, that's as may be, but you're OK. Don't lapse into a stupor again. Having got this far; keep it up.

I don't know why but the contact is not so good today; I'm finding it harder but just wanted you to know I'm still around and kicking.

Tell Arthur (*his friend*) I'll get to him in due course – he's got to take his turn. I've had as much as I could handle with Sheila to cope with – she's a handful and no mistake – doesn't give me a minute's peace!!!

As for being bored here, I've hardly had a chance to find out as I keep being called back by the Missus. Never mind, joking apart; I can be in several places at once, so it's no hardship.

I'm looking into Varna's case (*she had a stroke when she was twenty-two*). There are complications and hold-ups from the past which have contributed to her condition. Salt baths – Spa water would be helpful, as well as relaxation classes and seeing a dietician. The problem is vascomuscular. She lacked certain minerals as a child. I am asking the healers to look to her. She can be helped and her courage is noted. She has experienced a lot and has really overcome so much. As she becomes more open to the possibility of the unseen levels, she will be more in tune with healing forces.

Send her picture to Barbara. Healing comes in many forms and absent healing will do just as well as laying on of hands.

You could take her to see the healers at Whitley Bay too. It is a condition which has taken a hold over a long time and so will need regular healing sessions but there will be a marked improvement.

Arthur is soon going to find out there's more in Heaven and earth than he's dreamed of. Keep an open mind, Arthur, you'd be surprised how much you can learn and achieve if you do that. If you don't understand, go and seek out books and read. In time, you'll discover the truth for yourself. I wish I'd taken the trouble. I lived for the day but I could have helped myself so much if I'd had more knowledge.

Never mind, I'm doing OK and Sheila is really getting down to brass tacks. She won't know herself in a couple of years; she will have learned so much. She has lots to give and will. She'll be a real comfort to many people. You ain't seen nuffing yet! Keep tuning in; all love, Ralph.

23rd March 1988

I've been itching to get going – know it's not your day and you've got a lot to do, but please, just a short note to Sheila and I'll let you alone.

So pleased the baby is here safe and sound – it was a good delivery. I was there all the time and felt I was assisting the doctors. Varna has stood up to it well and will grow stronger day by day. She's being given a good deal of strength and will withstand this extra burden on her system.

Well, the little one is doing fine – no worry. Just keep your peckers up and know all works out for the best. The little 'hic-up' will soon settle down; there's nothing to worry about, just a little weakness at first but soon to clear up. I want to give my love and thanks to Varna and Arthur. They've been towers of strength to Sheila and I don't know what she'd have done without them. Of course, she's lucky to have Tim too; he's a great kid. I told you I'd get round to Arthur in time and I know he's been hard put to make head or tail of how these 'letters' come about. It's really very simple, though not so easy to put into operation. At first, I found it hard but then I got the hang of it and now I think it's great fun. And boy, do I enjoy my jaunts to Harrow. I'm not so sure about Barbara though. She certainly has her work cut out (*as a singer, costume designer, agent and artistic director of the Apollo Group of London, as well as singing for other companies and looking after her family and meditation students*) and often doesn't know if she's on her arse or elbow as she does so many different things and works between worlds.

Well, all I do actually is wish to communicate then I send that wish to Barbara and hope she'll pick up the link. That's how I'm working today. It is not her day for 'tuning in' and she's finding it difficult to spare time so I've been hanging around on the off-chance that I could get a word in. She's a good kid, so she's dropped everything to give me a few minutes. I mustn't outstay my welcome though. Anyway, having got her attention I bring my thoughts to synchronise with hers. At first, it's a difficult enterprise because our thoughts have to be so close that they merge, and the medium isn't always sure which is which. This is how misunderstandings can come about with mediums. It isn't that they want to cheat, far from it; most are decent, honest folk but the whole mechanism involves mind to mind and it's difficult to handle. Anyway, Barbara now has a lot of experience dealing with many people on many subjects, so she is able to keep her own mind pretty still and let mine come through. She could communicate with me in several ways but writing is a good record and she likes to see things on the page, especially as over a period, a clear picture emerges from the 'letters'.

You see, Arthur, I haven't really gone very far. I've only switched channels, so to speak. I am still in the same space but I live on a finer, higher, faster vibration, so I can't be seen with normal sight. However, on my own channel, I'm solid and so are things and people around me. I'm sure it's really all very scientific and more will be discovered about it because this is how it's got to be. So many people are scared of death but there's nothing to it; truly, it's smashing – I'm really enjoying myself and can't wait for you lot to join me. We'll have a swell time, believe me. But that's for a later day, of course; you've all got a lot of living to do on your own level and you've just become a new dad. It's really lovely and I envy you your dear little daughter. Give her a big hug from her Uncle Ralph and give Varna a big cuddle too, and tell her I'm proud of her – not half. Anyway, can't go on too long. Want a quick word with Shie.

Darling Shie, I'm so happy you're doing your best to keep chirpy; you're looking much happier and prettier too. You're a grand little trooper and you know I'm right by your side. I love our little chats and I'm sorry they seem a bit one-sided to you, but nevertheless, I do reply and gradually, you'll receive more and more of my thoughts. You could really develop your intuition very strongly. It's all there; you're really very psychic if you only try. Mind you, when I say try, I might mislead you; don't want to do that. Trying in the usual way can block; you can try too hard. Really it's as Barbara does, being very relaxed so that the mind quietens down and then allows things to enter. By staying open-minded, you release the mechanism which bridges the worlds.

The majority of people aren't aware of how much communication is open to them, yet where do you think inspiration comes from; where do you think poets, artists, musicians, scientists and writers, get their ideas, especially those incredible people sci-fi writers? Well, from other levels, of course. Nobody is only tuned into the physical channel, even if they think they are. No, it's often just called imagination but that's the gateway. Only those with a really active imagination can open the gateway but all receive information at some time from other levels. Usually, it is in the form of coincidence, or something inexplicable in the normal way, and they dismiss it.

Dreams also serve a purpose. Who hasn't occasionally had such a vivid dream that it seemed absolutely real? Well, it was. You, Arthur, for all you try to be down to earth and logical, have had some strange and puzzling dreams over the years, don't deny it. You sometimes instinctively know when something is going to happen and when it does, it shakes you rigid. Well, don't fear it, it's natural, but whether such things are pleasant or not depends on you. If you keep buoyant and optimistic, that's the world you tune into but if you are a pessimist, always looking on the black side, then that's where you'll fetch up.

It all depends on the individual. It seems a contradiction but though these worlds are real, we determine which we gravitate to. I've no complaints; I live in a really swell area – no litter, no louts; just warm, sunny and beautiful (like my Sheila, bless her). Don't let her get in the dumps. She's a silly chump when she does 'cos that comes between us; it's like a foggy, wet night when she gives way to grief, but when she talks to me and gives me a mental hug, all is warm and lovely again.

Must go, Barbara has to type this yet and has an extra lesson to give before going out to teach tonight. I know just what's going on here as well as at home. I like this house. It's full of life and light and colour. At present, she's concerned about Chris who is under the weather. She's got a lot of sorting out to do with him but I can see it's not serious and he'll pull through.

God bless you all, my darlings. I send my best to all my chums both home and abroad and do tell them I'm not dead but full of beans and living in two worlds at once. They'll think you're daft, of course, but who cares – I'm so full of life, I could chuck a pig over Percy Park.

I'll be back, never fear; I hear Barbara groan, "I'll get writer's cramp."

All love, Ralphie Pooh.

30th March 1988

I have to just shove in my 'four penneth' and say "hello," to Sheila and Tim and to say "ciao," to my friends from Genoa, Johnny and Carla.

So glad they are able to come to England and to see Shie. It will cheer her up a lot to see them and to remember old times; we have certainly had some fun together. Do you remember all the old trips and how we used to go off into the hills together on lovely, rosy evenings, drinking Chianti and all those lovely Italian wines at wayside inns and pubs? And the food – well, it used to blow us out but Shie didn't have to worry – didn't put on an ounce; whilst yours truly would have ended up like Friar Tuck on that sort of menu. But lovely it was, and I want Shie and Tim to take up those trips again when they feel able and I'll be along for the ride.

Well, have a good time and remember I'm around. You have given us great hospitality and it's always a treat for us to do likewise – we are pals of a life-time. We certainly go back a long way together. Love to Graziella and the family. Say "ciao" for me!

Now, young Tim; thought you were forgotten, did you? Well, can't deal with everything in one afternoon, and hardly felt I needed to mention your triumph as I knew all about it, being there, helping you along.[83] Young scallywag, thought you did it all by yourself, did you? Well, I'll have you know, you've got a deal to thank me for. Yes, I've been on all your trips and will continue to do so, until you have more experience; then I'll leave you to get on with it. Don't want to cramp your style but know I'm always within earshot and if you need me, just give a call and I'll be there.

Now, don't give in to Sheila and do all the driving; make sure she keeps her hand in too – and watch the brandy bottle; don't let her get pickled, whatever

---

[83] Apparently he had passed his driving test.

you do. But, joking apart, I'm so glad she's picking herself up. Only she can do it but you've been a tower of strength, old chap, and I'd hate to think how she'd have been without you. You're a good kid and a brave one and I salute you.

Have fun in London and don't stint yourselves. You'll soon earn the reddies to cover your spree – all work and no play, etc.

Now Shie, you're being a bit over sensitive regarding Arthur. He didn't mean to go off the handle but has been under a good bit of strain himself. Realise everybody has their inner struggles. You are able to verbalise yours but it puts a strain on other people when they are also trying to cope with life. Their concerns may not seem as serious as yours but everybody feels that their own troubles are the biggest, and some are not able to get things off their chest as you are; so just get on with your own life – know I'm around to comfort you and plod on.

Remember, laugh and the world laughs with you; cry and you cry alone. Keep chipper and enjoy your friends and let them enjoy you. Stop wearing your heart on your sleeve and people will come around you again. Being miserable sure drives people away and really, what have you to be miserable about when you know I'm alive and kicking and always with you?

Being able to get these messages across is a real act of grace but you must realise that I have to register on my own level. I have a new life to make – be with me in partnership and not just as a burden for me to carry. We each now have to develop our own individuality, and when we meet again we will both have progressed in the same way – you on your channel – me on mine. Then we will be able to move on together and won't that be marvellous?

If you are able to stand on your own feet you help me, as well as yourself, and I have to learn to be self-sufficient too. Of course, I miss you. I wish I could talk to you on my own level but I accept that this is how we have to be for the time being but are lucky to have our link. If you rely on me for everything and keep pulling at me, you unbalance me. Remember earth is a school and you now have to learn the lesson of detachment. It is a hard one but you can do it, and believe me, your values over the next few years will change drastically and you'll see what I mean.

You'll find enjoyment in many different ways and will realise that things which you think important now are not, while others are, and you'll settle into a lovely, rosy sunset of life with your hand in mine – not separate but beautifully moulded together, despite our different worlds. Isn't that a lovely and wonderful picture – you and me as Darby and Joan connected by a rainbow bridge of love? It beats eating fish and chips on a Friday night!!

Well, my love, I am aware of your trials, but seen from my side they're quite small ones, you know, and that is not to put you down. I know you're upset at Marg going[84] but really it's for the best and only so you can have somebody better. You're going to get busier in many ways and you need someone really efficient who will be seen but not heard! Also, you'll be able to bring out your best china without fear of ructions.

---

[84] I presume this was her cleaner

Give Tim my congrats. He's doing a great job and will become a good driver – 'cos he's got the best teachers around, especially now I can see around corners! Think that's all for now. As usual, I've jumped the queue. Best love to all at home; Varna, Arthur, baby, Fred and Rob, and all who remember me kindly. I'll see you in my dreams, dear Shie. All love, Ralph.

PS There's a great force in the universe that answers all prayers and calls for help. Don't try to make me play God. When you are in need, call on that supreme presence; that is the place where we all link, and you will be brought more strongly to me through that force. Name it what you will but know you can never be cut off from it, and the more you call on it in love and thanks, the more blessed we will be. It is easy on earth to feel separate from it but in truth, we never can be; we just don't think about it but from where I am – I actually feel the presence and see the light it carries, and I know this is where I have my life and being. Excuse me, speaking so seriously, but I know a bit more; not a lot, just a bit more than I did even a short time ago.

24th May 1988

Darling Shie, I'm overjoyed to be able to communicate again in the old way. I've never left you but you had to be allowed to discover your own strength and to stand firm in your own light; not that reflected by me.

This is the first time since we married that you've had to rely on your own strength and see what a good job you've made of it. My heart bursts with pride to see how you've coped and are coping. Yes, of course, some days are worse than others, but you have accepted and by so doing you are assured of making progress. This is all to the good because you've no time to lose in settling down to your new life. Lots of interesting things are opening up for you now and there is no time to lose because you'd hold yourself back from many good things. I'm so chuffed that you've made a start in your spiritual development and Tim also has a lot to give and a lot to gain.

Several doors will close but many more are due to open, and the fact that I am not there in my physical state is the only disappointment for you. However, you are embarking on the most fulfilling and interesting part of your life now.

It makes me smile when I hear you say that you'll never enjoy life again – little do you know what is stored up for you. I have been pounding light and strength into your aura and I am sure you have felt it. It's great that you've been able to put on such a good show in company. They all know how forsaken you feel; you don't have to spell it out 'cos they always knew we were a couple. There haven't been many better partnerships than ours and it goes on. We complement each other – I am able to keep in touch with your world through my link with you and in your sleep state you are already becoming familiar with my world of light; this is a large measure of your strength.

I told you there would be more 'letters' but this is not only for your benefit but to bring light and knowledge to others. It helps Barbara too and she's been feeling very bereft lately. She couldn't understand the closing down. She's been blaming herself but this had to be. You, as I say, had to learn to feel your feet and stop feeling sorry for yourself.

It's been a test of your faith and belief; firstly in my continued existence, then in the power of a source greater than both of us. Well, you've passed with flying colours – so now, we can take up the link again. Barbara's faith has also been tested at this time. She has been down a dark tunnel but will soon see the light at the end again.

I told you I'd arrange someone at your end and Hazel fits the bill nicely. She is a woman of substance and very sincere. She is no sensationalist and is not pursuing personal glory. Her energies are linking up with you and Tim at home, and Barbara in London, and will produce a good wattage (yes, it is very like an electrical circuit) and all to the good for yours truly to link with.

Mind you, this is not just to produce a club meeting for us; we are really setting up a vaster link than that in order for souls on your side and mine to be drawn to the power source to help those in need.

You see, it's not only those on your side who need help. Some people go on after death in much the same way they did in life and many are in a disorientated state. Well, a lot of us here are a bit more centred and try to help them. As they are close to earth vibrations we bring them into the orbit of centres of power, such as the one set up by Barbara and her Thursday group, and they are able to draw the vibrations into their energy fields. So they find more balance and then can take the stronger vibrations on our side better. There are so many wavelengths and I hope I'm managing to convey to you something of my meaning. I know it's a bit complicated for you but take my word for it – you're doing a grand job when you combine your energies and work for the Light. You, Sheila, have had a marvellous training in colour – now use it in the esoteric way as Barbara does. You have the colours of a healer in your energy field.

As Tim develops he will constitute a source of power to back yours. I don't mean power in the usual earthly sense but as a source of energy which is used for healing. You are at the threshold of a great learning experience, believe me. You will learn in so many ways, not just from books, though they will help you to understand some of the unfamiliar terms etc.

Your emotional strength in relation to Varna is being tested.[85] Stand firm and do not be 'manipulated' by her. She can be very dogmatic in her own right and she is very mixed up at the moment so is looking for a scapegoat. Refuse to be goaded. Go about your own business and let her get on with it. She knows where you are when she needs you.

Just like you, she has to sort herself out; you can't do it for her. She's made her bed and must lie on it. Naturally, I feel sorry for her, but we tried to warn her, didn't we? She sees the less glamorous side of the affair now. Children tend to cut one down to size.

---

[85] Ralph and Sheila loved Italy and always took their holidays there. They became friends with Varna's family when she was a little girl and she became a surrogate daughter to them, coming to stay at their home then moving to England and marrying an Englishman.

Anyway, if she contacts you, be as sweet as you always are, but don't be her doormat – OK? Arthur, of course, is part of the trouble – he's jealous of your influence on Varna and in little ways tries to stir trouble between you. Refuse to be drawn and let them get on with it – they deserve one another.

Now, dear love, I'll say goodnight. Love me ever, as I love you and take care of that dear boy. He is as dear to me as if he were my own son. As yet, I have no evidence, but deep in my heart, I believe he has certainly been so in some other time and place with me. I love you all. Remember me – I'm always close by. Your lover, (the one and only) Ralph.

Chapter Twenty
Ralph Learns More

4th October, 1988

Hello, dear Coz, Well met! Some time since we've had the chance of a chat. Now, here I am, high, wide and handsome.

Sheila is full of beans – no doubt but that she is doing a grand job. She is full of spunk and really trying to live a fulfilled and energetic life. Tell her I love her but she knows that anyway. I am full of beans to be able to get in touch again.

You have a lot on your plate at the moment and more coming up. You'll cope, never fear. Hasten slowly – that's true for us as well as you. We also have work to do but it's work we enjoy, nobody forces us into it; we decide what's best for us and get on with it. There are lots of experts over here – there's nothing one can't learn with a bit of effort.

Well, I've met up with a few old pals and family. I can't say I was that close to any of them on earth (only Aunt Rose) but that hasn't made any difference here. They were all pleased to greet me and have been kind – showing me the ropes and keeping me interested. It's like setting a child free in a sweet shop. Gosh, there certainly are lots of possibilities – it is mind boggling and no mistake. It takes a while to feel your feet – you just fly everywhere at first and the colours have to be seen to be believed. We are all free to experience what we like. We are not restricted but can find ourselves wherever we are fit to go.

I was in 'fairy-land'; it's all so beautiful, with so many things you've just never dreamed of. I am lost for words – I feel I want to pour my heart out, but am so limited, there's no vocabulary because there are no similarities on earth. Well, not that you can see at any rate – they're just out of range for you but we're not restricted; we not only see them but are amongst them.

Well, I kept feeling Sheila tugging at me but I didn't want to be bothered. Don't get me wrong. I love her dearly, but she was drawing me back into all the trivia and unpleasantness of the earth when I was in 'fairy-land'.

Perhaps it was good for me because I had to think about her and her plight. It made me realise how much we rely on other people when really we should learn to stand on our own feet. It is good to have their support but we mustn't stand in the light of another – not at all.

Now, I can restrict myself to my own plane, if I will, but I try to link from time to time with Sheila and Tim, though sometimes I forget. Sheila is not so insistent now so I feel free.

She's a good lass but so dependent on me that I felt like a drowning man. It is great that she's learning to cope and accept. In that way, we can be two free individuals – devoted but not claustrophobic to each other. Please don't show her this – it would upset her, but you understand and are learning what it is to be singular in intent.

Gosh, but it's all so paradoxical, isn't it? We strive on earth to find an ideal partnership and then have to try to transcend it. I'm doing my best but not always in balance.

Anyway, to get down to brass tacks, I'm now starting what I was due to accomplish on earth but couldn't because of my rocky old body. I did delay; if only I'd become aware earlier, but there it is, no good complaining now, so I have to make up for lost time.

I shall assist your Chris – not just me, of course, but a group of us being taught by higher beings who understand health matters and healing. He has had a lot to cope with in niggling ways, but if he hadn't, he'd never have built up a resistance to disease and a compassion for sufferers. He would have been harder and somewhat dismissive of illness. As it is, he feels strongly for those who suffer and will be led to those he can help.

His uncle *(Reg)* would appreciate his company more; not necessarily chatting but just giving support and calm, especially after the silly chatter of the ladies *(Reg's sisters)*.

There is such a lot of work waiting for us all. Sheila is also part of our team – which stretches pretty far. She will be involved with a group in her area as you are in yours. Gradually, all these small groups will link and the power from the combined forces will be enormous.

It's a slow game but so rewarding. It's the caring that matters – from that standpoint we'll be guided and more intensive training will be given. You and Chris ain't seen nuffing yet! There is so much information and wisdom to come through as you get more ready for it.

We are able to draw in close now and your teachers are ever at your side. You, Barbara, will be used more and more as a channel for them. You are the mouthpiece but a lot of healing will come through Chris. It is a real combination and as one needs a build-up, the other will supply it – with the aid of the 'watchers', of course. This is very much a training period; Barbara, you are the teacher and Chris is the healer.

The trouble with many healing groups has been the amateurism. There needs to be an assessment made. People need not expect to get treatment for free if they can afford to pay. All will be pooled and shared. Centres must be run to pay their way. The downfall of many groups has been lack of organisation and woolly mindedness. Nobody is saying rook people and make a fortune or take people for a ride, but treat the matter as a profession. Cover costs but give value for money and those who can pay will pay, but there should be concessions for those who can't.

It's important to get this money thing sorted out. So many 'good' people think it's not nice but it's the coinage of the earth. The days of barter are gone.

All need to pay their bills. The 'Powers' who bring forth these gifts give freely to those who've earned them, but that's OK because we don't deal in money here. You all have to live so no being silly and feeling it a virtue to starve in the gutter. No need for that, you'll be looked after if you give service, but you can't leave it all to us – we don't dwell on the earth plane.

Anyway, just thought I'd put you both in the picture. Can't thank you enough for what you did for Sheila and me. It's great that we can all still correspond, despite all being at different levels. Actually, the higher you go, the more becomes available to you. I'm determined to keep moving on. I'm really on my way to the stars – you bet!

We only have to think of somebody and we tune in with them. I've been quite amused at your dad's progress. From being as miserable as sin, he's now having a whale of a time and will soon realise what a lot he can contribute through music. He doesn't just have to keep it to himself. At first, he was making up for lost time because when he realised he had the chance to really take music seriously, it just took him over. He's enjoyed it to a much deeper extent than he did on earth. He was always a bit casual about it then. Anyway, he's doing fine and will soon learn that he can join with us and bring us some very potent vibes, thanks to the sounds he's producing.

Tim is a good lad and I love him dearly and he is becoming aware of other worlds. Just keep an eye on both of them and make sure they don't get mixed up in mumbo-jumbo or superstition, which is always the danger in Spiritualist or religious circles. Recommend some good books or let them see the teachings now and again.

From where I am, I see that there's a lot more to come through to you, with the emphasis on healing and magnetism. Love from us all – keep smiling – all is fine. Love, Ralph.

This turned out to be Ralph's last 'letter' in this form. He moved on further but Sheila had come to rely on the letters and was upset because I didn't keep them going. She didn't realise that unless my 'telephone' rang I could do nothing. There had to be someone at the other end of the line. Sheila should have been grateful that Ralph had been in contact for almost two years, but he was not allowed to go on being her crutch indefinitely.

Rather than being pleased for what she had received, she thought I was letting her down.

However, she and Tim began going regularly to the local Spiritualist Church, met people with the same interests and began their spiritual journey. They worked together in her firm until it was sold and Sheila went into a residential home, where she died peacefully at the age of ninety-one. Tim married, had two children, and when I last heard from him, was doing well as an accountant in Newcastle.

Chapter Twenty-One
Greetings

18th October 1988, *my son's eighteenth birthday.*

Dear Friends, we greet you on this day of days – a turning point for the young man, as he goes from childhood into adulthood and maturity.

He is set on an interesting and unique pathway and is guarded and guided on his journey. He has nothing to fear – merely to look upwards to the light and let it guide him.

We've come as a group to bring our wishes, love and hope to him, and to let him know there are many gathered around him this day from the planes of light. His is the way of the determined disciple of light – forget it not. Know that the pathway is lit for him and was from before the moment of his birth.

Go forward unhampered and let your very soul lead you onwards, dear one. There is much to be achieved but do not become impatient – know all happens in its own good time.

You will have many fine colleagues and never want for a friend. Life will become ever more interesting so look forward to it jubilantly, loyally and courageously. All is well. Enjoy your celebration; it is the first of many. Love and light is all around you. This is your majority and there are many to share it with you on both sides of the curtain. If you do not know them all, that does not matter; they know you, and through your parents, many have drawn near and have become aware of you.

Never despise the work that goes forward in this house (*meditation group and healing*) it is bringing love and comfort to so many and is providing you with a firm background from which your own work will be generated. There are numerous levels of light blending to make contributions to your celebrations.

Your grandfathers, Harold and Albert are overjoyed to link with you, as are your maternal grandparents.

Go forth, young warrior of the light – your path is illumined and glorious is the dawn.

We send our love and thanks to you all. Ralph has just caught up and asks not to be forgotten.

24th October 1988

The next communication was from a group led by Greg and intended for my family and friends.

Hello Everybody,

Well, isn't this fun; who'd have thought such a thing was possible. I told you we would be together, but you didn't believe me. Well, here we are to prove it. If only you could feel how privileged and overjoyed we are. It is impossible to convey the feeling we have. Ralph and Albert are here, Ted, and Dorothy's mum. There are so many of us. Sheila's mum and dad and all the others send their love. We are all like a crowd around a telephone box but only one can speak at a time. Well, Barbara, you've got your work cut out to cope, but sure you will.

Anyway, we just want you all to know we're proud of you; the way you have accepted that we're not 'dead'. In our own world, we are totally alive and you are keeping us alive in yours. It is great to know.

We will see you're alright. You have no need to fear or dread loneliness. You are never alone unless you really desire to be. Just sit quietly when you feel depleted or overcome with life's troubles. Send out a call to us and know that we can tune in immediately and bring warmth and love.

Talk over your problems with us *(telepathically)* and because we can see more than you do; we can help calm your fears and bring a sane conclusion to the problem.

When you are depressed, call on us and we'll bring light and refreshment to you. You don't have to bear your troubles alone, you know. You will be given more opportunities now that you are waking up to the realities of real life; the combination of the material aspect with the spiritual.

Know that all goes ahead in the great scheme of things. It is only through the work of groups such as yours that the world's balance and salvation will be brought about. It is not to politicians and the establishment that society should look. No, it is the bringing forth of light and healing by ordinary human beings – that is the salvation to come.

Believe in the truth and know all is working out for the best. Yes, there'll be hardship for many but if they won't learn any other way, that's how it has to be.

You are all being given the opportunity to do all you can to wake people up to reality.

Ralph takes over: Well, tell Sheila I'm really proud of her; my heart just bursts for joy and I'm delighted at Tim's progress. What a terrific kid he is. Albert is likewise proud of the girls, and Dorothy has given him hope and heart at the way she has responded since she's been in this house (*in Harrow*); having a laugh and being brighter than she's been for months. Keep up the good work.

We are pumping up the energies and learning a lot ourselves too. Right, we'd love to go on but must withdraw. Barbara is dealing with potent energy.

It's been great hearing you talking about us all so kindly and lovingly today, and glad you appreciate and enjoy the 'letters'. We enjoy sending them. Till next time – keep chipper.

All love, Ralph, Albert, and the gang.

25th May 1990

For respite, I stayed for a few days at the Seeker's Trust at Addington Park, near Maidstone. It is situated on an old, wooded estate with a lake and pre-historic remains in the vicinity. At the entrance gate, almost hidden in undergrowth, is a sign – 'Merlin's Brook'. A small group of residents live in delightful cottages and there is a library, six healing chapels where absent healing takes place each day, at specific times, linking with people in their own homes around the world, and a conference hall where I first heard Peter Dawkins speak. There is also a rose garden in which the bereaved commemorate their departed loved ones by planting a rose and each year there is a Rose Festival Day. A number of small cottages are available for guests who wish to enjoy the tranquillity of the place.

I had been there several times with my meditation group; my husband and a friend from France, but I also appreciated being alone. I spent a good deal of time in meditation, read in the library and walked in the woods, replenishing my spiritual energies and resting my physical body. I was also interested in the pre-historic remains in the area and on one occasion, I walked over fields with my friend and pianist, Jillian Skerry, to the Coldrun Stones, close to the Pilgrim's Way leading to Canterbury. We intoned notes at random but found that when our voices accidentally coincided on the intervals of a fourth, fifth or octave, we felt a surge of energy.

In Medieval music, these were important intervals and perhaps they had earlier origins in a science of sound. In fact, church chantries, although now used for prayers for the dead, may have had their origins in places where energies were generated by sound and stored. We still have a great deal to learn about the technologies of our ancient ancestors and there is a vast field of research awaiting modern scientists regarding the science of sound, of which we have merely touched the surface.

The following 'letter' was received during my meditation at Addington:

Hello, Barb, dear old Codger. Good on yer for trying. What a smooth ride, wasn't it? You're so surrounded by lovely light and calm vibes that it's much easier than usual to reach you. Lovely smooth transition – thanks – these healing energies are the real thing and the best sort of healing colours are playing all around you in this place.

It's a lovely area and the energies have been well handled because they are not just stored up and then left but used every day and there is a wonderful coming and going and co-operation between your realm and ours.

Well, Pop Albert *(my father)* is with me and we're so glad you've taken the time to link with us. We're certainly trying hard to get some sense into those girls *(Albert's granddaughters)*. It's a tough job, as you know but we don't give up so easily and will keep pumping power into them. It's a deep seated trauma and will take a while to work through – also, they're both very stubborn and have to realise things for themselves before they take notice. Don't despair, just keep the prayers going; there's nothing more you can do at this juncture. We'll support them with all the light we can muster, though we can only send a bit at a time because they couldn't absorb the full force.

Yes, Martin is a tower of strength (*he was the boyfriend of one of them*) all force to him – we'll see he's OK.

Now, what about you? What's this, sitting on our 'letters'? We want you to get them out and about. It's all very well you receiving them but we want them circulated. You've sat on them for too long. Get them into print and out into the public domain. That's where they'll be really useful. We have to write through your mind and fingers, and those of others like you; we know your reservations but these are simply tools to help raise human consciousness.

Your path is being cleared to give you time to write and organise yourself. You don't have to give up singing but you can combine it with your spiritual work. You won't be left destitute but please take the time offered.

26th May 1990

The previous letter continued the following day. I had twisted my ankle getting off a bus on my way to Addington and it was still painful.

Sorry about the pain but we've been working on it during the night and that has stirred things up a bit making it more sensitive and painful. Bear with us; we will not leave you stranded. Your legs are indeed important to you and we will endeavour to keep them strong.

Go on your way in good faith; know that you are supported physically and metaphysically so you have nothing to fear. We always support God's messengers. You would not be kept here if you did not have work to do.

We do not feed you too much information in case you get indigestion from realising all that is to be accomplished in the remaining years.

Go forward a day at a time. That is your discipline. A good soldier has to learn discipline. You will be prompted whenever there is a job to be done but you are now beginning to realise that energy needs to be conserved. That is a universal law; God is not prodigal with energy. You will gradually see more clearly what is to be done or avoided.

Just know that you are never alone; always your guardians accompany you. You are monitored and it is known when you need rest to recharge your store of energy. The batteries in your tape recorder get worn down, and in the same way, your physical mechanism needs recharging. Times of quiet are necessary for your higher consciousness to link so that you become aware of the next stage of the journey.

You are now beginning to understand that your work does not just involve what you do on a physical level. Your music has been important because it has enabled you to send out energies into other planes (*the lower astral areas, I suspect*) to provide much needed light.

This new perspective should interest you because you are aware of the higher levels sending light into lower levels. However, with an awakened soul, the converse is true. All the time you thought you were planning a career and looking ahead – the principles of light and life were taking what you sent out into the 'ether' and used it in twilight zones. Many a poor, stranded soul is grateful to you, even though you were, from an earthly standpoint, hardly aware of this aspect. Thus, you are able to work in those lower, dense areas of poor light because you yourself have provided the means of lighting your way to help others who are still stumbling in the dark.

These souls are not all wicked; the majority are simply ignorant. They often had hard physical lives with no time to ponder the greater realities.

You do like to sit on the fence, though; a bit more courage is needed, you've nothing to lose and many have a lot to gain.

Later, my father and my cousin, Greg, took advantage of my pen.

Hello, Barb, my darling. So glad you've had these few days to sort yourself out and to think about the book or books, I should say, as there are more to come.[86] All we need is your commitment. You have never been a hundred per cent with us, though you have been interested and intrigued, you don't trust yourself enough.

We trust you; we know you as a truthful person, who is not concerned with personal gain but works with us as our amanuensis. We are many in number. I am only a humble spokesman because my case is similar to many who come over as I did, and also, our frequencies match perfectly through our type and our love links. We are very close in spirit and understand each other very well.

I am casting off my dross and am amazed to find a colourful and bright sheen underneath. I am not as base as I was painted (by myself). There is merit from other lives too and I've learned to forgive myself and grow.

I love the opportunity to expand into the light. It is worth all the suffering to know, really know, what is involved and to absorb the rays of colour right into the soul of my being.

We are surrounded, if we only knew, by colour, wonderful worlds of light and heavenly guardians. Well, I know now and am not losing any time to take advantage of what's on offer. Greg is a great character. I like him a lot. He is a dear friend to me. I wasn't aware of him at first because I was so wrapped up in myself but he quietly observed me and patiently waited till I was ready to respond, and so we became good friends. He has a great sense of humour – is no respecter of persons and really ribs some of the pompous busybodies who come over here. But beyond all this, his is a heart of gold and silver, and he has a deep understanding of the human condition.

I see that I have to rest you for a while; signing off now in love and light, Dad and Greg.

From 1980 until 1985, I was involved each summer with the Opera Festival in Munich and in 1983, I was in my hotel room packing my case, before leaving

---

[86] A reference to a compilation of the 'post mortem letters'.

for Salzburg and, naturally, was fully occupied with what I was doing. Suddenly, however, the following words literally dropped into my head.

BEYOND TIME; BEYOND SPACE; BEYOND CONSCIOUSNESS; ONLY A ONENESS OF BEING, THAT IS GOD.

One night in 1985, I dreamed that I was on a film location but not as a performer. I was with a very large man with sandy hair and a full beard, a veritable Viking. It was a very lucid dream and I remembered it when I awoke. I told Chris about it but he said he couldn't see how I would be involved with a major movie of that kind. Nevertheless, a few weeks later, a girl named Sally, whom I had met when our son, Giles, was on location with the TV Series 'Drummonds', asked me if I was busy for the next couple of weeks. As it happened, there wasn't anything important going on so when she asked me if I could help her out by becoming a chaperone for a young lad, Sid Owen, on location in Norfolk; I agreed. A chaperone's permit was rushed through for me and off I went to join the film crew. Sid was playing Al Pacino's son in 'Revolution' and the location started in King's Lynn. He was then fifteen and new to filming. He did not find it easy but Al Pacino took him under his wing and the 'Viking' I had met in my dream, the actor turned dialogue coach, Robert Easton, devoted a great deal of time to working with him. Robert and I got on famously, and he even came to have dinner with us in Harrow when filming ended. He was fascinated by Chris's Uncle Reg who was over from Jersey, as he had the genuine accent of a Middlesex farmer. While having coffee after dinner, Robert made copious notes in phonetics, just like Professor Higgins in 'Pygmalion'.

There were also two Native American actors, an older man, Skeeter Vaughan and Graham Greene, who later appeared with Kevin Costner in 'Dances with Wolves'. While Sid was filming, I spent a lot of time in the catering bus chatting to these three men and learned a lot about Native American culture and the film business.

Seeing how King's Lynn was transformed into an 18th-century port was fascinating, as well as seeing the very large number of extras in costumes of the period. The cast was star studded, led, not only by Pacino, but also Donald Sutherland, who was very relaxed with the extras between battle scenes. Nastasya Kinsky, a very modest girl, was the love interest, and such experienced British actors as John Wells, Robbie Coltrain, Andrew Ray, Joan Plowright and many others from stage and screen turned up for their own particular parts in the filming.

I often used to sit quietly in Ely Cathedral when filming took place nearby and when the unit moved down to Plymouth for filming on Dartmoor I went with them. However, I had my own work to return to so could not remain on location all the time. Nevertheless, there were occasional days when I was not busy so I accompanied children either to Plymouth or to King's Lynn for filming. It was a most interesting experience. I was more used to TV filming but seeing such a

large movie coming to fruition was captivating. Hugh Hudson was the director and David Putnam the producer. However, Hudson said that he left his film on the cutting room floor. The powers that be wanted the film to make the Academy Awards so it was rushed through. I recently saw it on TV and thought it a better film than originally reviewed. As I had been mainly involved with the exterior scenes, it was interesting to see all the interior ones and the actors that I had not been aware of who
were in the cast.

Later that year, Chris and I, with Frances Gregory and Jillian Skerry, were singing in the Pump Room in Bath and Lord Putnam was in the audience. Although only fifteen, Giles was filming the concert for us and in the interval Lord Putnam spoke to him and asked him about his equipment. I don't think though that Giles mentioned that his mum had been on location with his film unit. It is a funny old life.

Chapter Twenty-Two
Another Decade

For me, the 1980s had been a decade of incredible spiritual and metaphysical awareness but as if to restore balance, from 1990 onwards, I was returned to mundane conditions with a bump. I had been told that a lot of challenges lay ahead and they certainly did.

Everything was changing and the Apollo Group of London which we had run since 1965 gradually went into abeyance. I sang in 'Madame Butterfly' and 'Eugene Onegin' in Lille and 'Onegin' in Marseilles. My last solo role was as Elvira in 'Don Giovanni' for a company in Hastings when I was fifty. Then, in 1988, Chris and I were engaged for the first arena opera, a magnificent spectacle of 'Aida' transported from the Verona Arena in Italy, which opened at Earl's Court in London and in the indoor Arena in Birmingham. This was followed by productions of 'Carmen' and 'Tosca' in London, Japan, Germany and Switzerland throughout the early 90s. Chris also sang in Marseilles, Bordeaux, Nice; with the Netherlands Opera in Amsterdam, as well as at the Monnaie Theatre in Brussels, and in Antwerp. Giles and I often joined him for a long weekend but, where possible, he also commuted between performances.

In 1992, we moved to Stanmore and developed a successful singing teaching practice in our new home. I also continued singing recitals with Jillian Skerry and we sometimes gave concerts with Chris. He continued singing solo roles with various companies in London and the provinces and I became an adjudicator at competitive music festivals around the country.

I was still a member of the College of Psychic Studies and in one class an American student told me that psychically he saw me laden with mountains of paper and predicted that I would do a lot of writing. I was very sceptical but his clairvoyance has proved true.

From 1989, Jillian Skerry and I went to France every year and, purely out of interest I began to learn about the life of Pauline Viardot Garcia, the sister of Maria Malibran. As a result of this, I was asked by Dr Alexandre Zviguilsky of the Amis d'Ivan Tourgueniev, Pauline Viardot et Maria Malibran, at Bougival, on the outskirts of Paris, to write a monograph of Viardot's English career. It was a case of where Angels fear to tread because when I returned to England, I found I had to become a detective because there was little material in English in the public domain, apart from April Fitzlyon's 1964 book which was out of print. However, I got stuck in and discovered material in French as well as various diaries and reviews in English. The monograph was eventually published in

French and I began receiving letters from scholars around the world, who encouraged me to write a biography.

Fortunately, as a singer, I had a working knowledge of French, German and Italian, and read the Cyrillic alphabet, having sung in Russian, so it was not as big a hurdle as it might have been. I also realised that I had the instincts of a detective and even discovered original material.

The deaths of my nieces from anorexia deeply affected the family, not least my mother who had brought them up. She had been subject to years of stress and finally, it resulted in serious illness. She was admitted to Hartland's Hospital in Birmingham and I used to visit her each week. After some time, she returned home but one Sunday morning my sister, Mary, rang me to say that Mum's partner, Dan, had found her in a coma. I immediately caught a train to Birmingham and was soon at her bedside with the rest of the family. She had come out of the coma but had undergone several stringent tests which exhausted her and she was now under sedation. The medics said they had made her comfortable but gave no hope of recovery. She was eighty-six and her heart and all her organs were failing. She was in a deep sleep but we stayed until 11.30 pm and were then advised to go home though the hospital would let us know if there was a change. I bent over her and told her how much we loved her and that we appreciated what a good mother and grandmother she had been to us but now she could fly free with our blessing. I went back with Mary to her flat but we could not sleep so sat talking. At 2.30 am the phone rang to say that Mum had gone. It was very sad yet we were glad that her physical suffering was over.

Mum's brother-in-law, Jack, had died two days before but she was too ill to be told. I went back to Birmingham for the funeral with Chris and Giles and gave a short eulogy. We then returned home to Stanmore.

A few months before my mother became ill, I was visiting our friends Ivan and Marguerite whose psychic friend, Jenny, was also there. I had never met Jenny before but as my ninety-two-year-old mother-in-law, May, was ill at the time, I asked Jenny if she could pick up any information about her as the doctors had not diagnosed her problem. She said she was sorry to tell me that it was my mother who only had a short time to live. I was quite sure that she was wrong but within a few months, she was proved right as May had an operation and lived for another three and a half years. It was my mum who became ill and died.

When we returned from Mum's funeral, I noted that there was to be a psychic fair in Stanmore Broadway so I booked a private sitting with a medium and she immediately said she could hear the sounds of a party with music and a lot of laughter. She then added, "Jack is there too."

My mother, who was a dance pianist, always said that she would have a big party when she "went over there". Now, it seemed that she was as good as her word, though when she died she did not know that Jack had predeceased her.

About a year afterwards, we were having supper with our friends Susie and George when Susie, a gifted healer and medium, asked me to give her my wedding ring to psychometrise.

Suddenly she said, "I have to do this" and flung her hands up and down an imaginary keyboard just as Mum had done on the piano. The movement was so characteristic of Mum that it seemed that she wanted us to know that she was still alive and kicking. However, I never received 'letters' from her the way I did from Dad and Ralph, and I was never aware of any contact with my nieces, though I prayed for them both before and after their deaths. They had really committed slow suicide over more than a decade which, I suppose, could have had an effect on their post mortem state.

Writing as well as teaching now began to take over my life, though I still gave recitals; however, it was not long before Chris's 90-year-old uncle Reg, who lived in Jersey, became very frail and had to go into a residential home. We all visited him as often as possible but latterly I went over once a fortnight in order to maintain his house and large garden. He died in 2001 and Chris and I moved permanently to Jersey in 2004.

My first volume of the Viardot biography was published in hardback in 2003 by Cambridge Scholars Press and was accompanied by a CD of me singing some of Viardot's own compositions with Jillian Skerry at the piano. The first edition was disappointingly presented so I put an embargo on it and bought in the copies already printed. In 2004, a revised edition appeared with a dust cover based on my own design.

During my visits to France with Jillian Skerry, I painted a great deal and continued to do so in Jersey, having installed a wooden hut in the garden as my studio, and in 2008 I had a solo exhibition at the Communicare Centre in Les Quennevais, which was opened by Kate Jennings of BBC Radio Jersey. Chris and I both broadcast a good deal, talking about opera and my various interests. I was also given some programmes where I selected music that meant a lot to me.

In 2010, I was invited to give a recital in commemoration of the centenary of the death of Pauline Viardot Garcia at Les Frenes, her estate at Bouglival, on the outskirts of Paris. The Viardot's great friend, the Russian writer, Ivan Tourgueniev, built a dacha in the grounds and that is now the Tourguenive Museum where concerts are held during the summer months. At Guildhall, Chris, Charles Robin Broad and I were like the Three Musketeers, and have remained great friends ever since. Robin is a very successful composer and performer who made his career in Germany and he came to Paris to play for me. The programme consisted of several of Viardot's own songs as well as those by her eminent friends, including Chopin, Liszt, Schumann and Gounod.

I finally retired from singing in 2012, after recording a group of songs for the BBC and singing at the BBC Carol Concert.

My academic publishers had now become Cambridge Scholars Publishers and I was asked to write a second volume of the Viardot biography. I had already acquired a large amount of research material so the second book came together much quicker than the first one. It was published in hardback in September 2012 and the paperback versions of both books were published six months later. I sang some of the Viardot songs for the first volume, and my son, Giles, sang a group of her songs for the second one.

In recent years, there has been a great deal of concern about ecological matters; especially the health of the earth and our place and purpose on the planet. The scientist, James Lovelock, named the earth, Gaia and declared that it is a living, conscious organism.

I was unaware of this concept when, about forty years ago, I was travelling to North Wales in a car with Chris and our pianist, Jillian Skerry, having given concerts at Torbay, on the south coast of England. Chris was snoozing and Jill, who was driving, was concentrating on the unfamiliar road. I was in the back of the car enjoying the scenery but not thinking of anything in particular when I became aware that my consciousness was expanding like a piece of elastic, and I seemed to be in communion with the earth as a living being. I don't know how long it lasted but I have never had such an experience again, though I remember how, as a young child, I often felt a great urge to merge with fields and forests on family drives in the country.

The following text was received on the 31st of January, 1996, more than twenty years after the previous experience.

"Dear Ones, Welcome to my heart – my lifeblood sings with joy at your compassion and love. I am very willing and happy to link with you to share my dreams and hopes for all my progeny.

"Children can be wilful, yet parents love them, whilst trying to direct them into better channels. Come what may, I love; therefore I suffer in experiencing the wilfulness of my dear ones. If they learn then it is not wasted, yet many do not and the suffering continues and spreads. Yet some are now waking up and listening, so I am hopeful.

"Of course, there are many who choose other ways, often out of fear as much as wilfulness, and yes, the urge for power causes much distress; yet there must be those who govern and organise at this stage of evolution. There cannot be wholesale anarchy; discipline is needed but should not be imposed; self-discipline is the answer.

"You ask what you can do. Simply more of what you are doing and thinking. Thoughts of love, wherever or at whatever they are directed are very beneficial; not only to those receiving directly but for myself and my progeny. Whatever you do with love is beneficial however trivial the pastime may be.

"Walking my woods, appreciating the natural world, linking with and thanking the unseen life forces; these give me joy and your direction of love towards me, your gratitude and good thoughts sustain and help me.

"The links of love and prayers for discarnate friends also help, leading to the cleansing of lower astral levels and the releasing of earthbound humans in distress.

"You are doing necessary work in your own area – do not feel you should be rushing around. Each one of you is being encouraged to care and nurture in their own neighbourhood. "When you are needed to go further afield, you will be notified and it will be arranged.

"You need not fear lack of money; it will materialise. Just keep faith and listen; go with the flow and stay in the Light of love. You will not go wrong.

"Respect others; give them their space and rights and recognise their will."

On the 27th of May, 1990 I received the following communication relating to healing.

"There is still misunderstanding about healing. It is good that there are true and loving hearts who wish to apply healing but there are dangers inherent in playing with energies you do not sufficiently understand.

"A loving heart is the first step. Without it, you would have no wish to help others.

"The most important thing is to receive help from the unseen forces. Your own energies would not be sufficient, and to channel an excess of energy could make both recipient and healer ill.

"It works this way – a loving thought or prayer brings forth a response from a relevant plane. An assessment of the problem and of the patient is made. No energy will be wasted; thus, if it is judged that the case would respond well to orthodox medical treatment – the extra healing energies will be withheld for use in more recalcitrant cases.

"The state of the healer is important because it takes a long time to prepare a physical body in order to bear the relevant charges of energy. A healer is a transformer – the intensity of energy has to be stepped down before it can safely be received by the patient.

"Occasionally there is a 'so-called' miraculous healing. This is when everything comes together and enables an instant healing to take effect. It is essential that the place, the state of health of the healer and the degree of spiritual development of the patient must synchronise. These ideal conditions are rarely found together.

"We know you sometimes have doubts and question the efficacy of healing. In many cases, too sudden a healing would delay the spiritual lesson that is to be learned then the condition would be useless as a tool of learning.

"Pain sensitises. In the best of all worlds, there would be no illness, no bodily difficulties but this is not the best of all worlds; it is a lowly school.

"There are complications regarding the blending of all the subtle bodies, plus mind. Your bodies have electrical circuits, plus fundamental memory patterns set up in babyhood, childhood and onwards. Habits also play a crucial part in relation to lifestyles, economic factors and downright abuses, such as over-eating, excessive drinking, drug-taking, smoking, etc. So you see, there are no fast and easy answers.

"You wish to help others to avoid suffering which is all to the good at a local level; yet in view of eternity, suffering is a drop in the ocean and will strengthen a soul, enabling it to enter the realms of light.

"Use your love and willingness to heal if you are asked but know that you are monitored. There is still something of the egoist in one who wants everything done immediately, and to prove to unbelievers that healing works.

"Just hasten slowly and know that your love and light is accepted, taken and used by wiser minds than yours.

"This is not a ticking off; just to put you in the picture and to relieve your mental quandaries.

In love and light: The Healers."

As we are only a few miles by sea from Brittany and Normandy, I go over to France from time to time to paint. There is a good TGV service to Paris via Rennes, so I do not need to be cut off even though I live on an island. As I have incarnated in France several times, I now know why I love it so much, even though I met my end in a grisly way near the end of the 18th-century, though not on the guillotine; that would have been a mercy, as it would have been quick. I have always been very wary of knives and now I know the reason.

I am thrilled to have opera available to us in Jersey, thanks to performances in HD from the Met and Covent Garden. Of course, though I am now merely a member of the audience, I naturally relive the performances Chris and I sang in operas in which we have appeared throughout our long careers and there is nothing like knowing an opera from the inside to really appreciate what is happening on stage.

We all have a story to tell and from my experience, I know that life doesn't end in the here and now. No knowledge or skill is wasted because it will be used somewhere at some time, even if not in our present life.

I have no wish to convert others; I can only speak candidly of my own experiences and let my communicators speak for themselves, but I know that when the time comes, my life as Barbara will only be the ending of a chapter, in order to open another one. It will be the same with all of us, whether we believe it or not. All I ask is that my readers keep an open mind and wait and see.

I began this book by writing of my first 'out of body' experience in 1973 when I was aware of being out in the Cosmos in telepathic communion with an unseen group. Now I know that they are the Elohim, spiritual forces watching and protecting earth and the life thereon. They guide and teach but as with toddlers learning to walk, do not pick us up every time we stumble. The Wise Ones know that we have to learn to walk and grow in our own light but the Divine Light is there for us forever and regardless of how often we fail, they are always there to guide and encourage us if we ask for their help, as we make our way up the steep hill of spiritual ascent to the place of everlasting life.

Chapter Twenty-Three
Postlude

I know that I have been male as well as female in past lives and in fact, the life after that of a nun was as a male prelate of high rank in the Roman Catholic Church who died in 1617 after five years of imprisonment. It was a difficult life because it involved handling power. However, a love of music and architecture softened the character. He lived in a province of Austria and I discovered his mausoleum in the Campo Santo of an old church. The strange thing was that when my son was about fourteen, an Austrian boy from the same city came to stay with us on a visit arranged by the school, and on our way back from picking him up at the airport, I casually asked him if he had heard of this prelate. Imagine my surprise, when the present he had brought me was a long-playing record with the portrait of the man in the dress of a cardinal, on the sleeve. The music had been performed at his ecclesiastical court where my dad said he had been a musician in an earlier incarnation: coincidence, or what?

There is no hard and fast rule about how often or how long are the periods in between returning to earth; that depends on the spiritual evolution of the entity. The intervals between my incarnations have not been very long but it all makes sense to me now. However, eventually, we are all meant to gain release from karma then we have the choice of returning to earth as benefactors or moving onto realms of Light.

Maria was my sister in the early 19th-century and we were both singers. The body from that life is buried in the cemetery of Montmartre in Paris and I have visited the tomb. It seems funny to stand in such a place while existing in another personality but illustrates the continuity of life. For the body, it is a case of dust to dust ashes to ashes but the eternal consciousness continues on its journey. I am now aware of some other lives, some in more detail than others, and with an extended perspective, I realise that my credo encapsulates goodness, truth and beauty.

In 2013, a friend from Yorkshire, another Jane, put me in touch with someone who had always loved opera. At the age of thirteen, she was living in Italy and met Maria Callas whom she found warm and friendly. As a result of meeting her and seeing her on stage, she developed a great admiration for her and we now believe that Maria was instrumental in influencing Jane, to bring us together.

Angelina, as I call her, told me about two books by Helena Hawley.[87] Although Hawley is not a singer, Maria Callas worked with her on sound healing from 2000 which is the subject of both books. Up to that time, I had not heard of Hawley or her books but they are an incredible confirmation of my experiences with Maria. We have now discovered that Angelina was also a singer in her immediate past life. She was named Mathilde and studied with Viardot, caring for her in the last three years of Viardot's life.

Although Angelina had always wanted to sing, she made her career in the equestrian world, just like Hawley but now that she is retired. She is taking lessons with our friend, Marian, who on retiring from performing, settled in Norfolk where she teaches. As luck would have it, she only lives a few miles from Angelina, so at the age of seventy, Angelina began a course of study with her. She is totally dedicated and practises every day so that her progress has been remarkable. She is now beginning to sing music by the great composers and has appeared in the chorus of Gluck's opera 'Orfeo' which was staged in Norwich. She also takes part in workshops held by established professional singers and teachers. If one has the desire, the dedication and capacity for taking pains, it is never too late.

Of course, she will not become a professional singer in this life but she has professional standards and with her newfound knowledge of past incarnations, she believes that she is preparing for a future life as a singer. By this token, it would appear that she did not achieve all she wished in her life as Mathilde so is willing to try again.

Each decade has brought me fresh experiences, both in the inner and outer worlds, and I look forward to more writing and painting, I gave up teaching when I moved to Jersey but writing is now my passion.

For a while I did not meditate regularly, though I continued praying and sending absent healing to those in need. I also painted prolifically. From time to time I had unusual experiences, including two profound visions which I painted; one of the Earth Mother and one of the Ancient of Days. This entity is of another realm of being and looks frightening in his physical form but when he conversed with me, I felt I was in the presence of a truly loving father. Many unorthodox historians and researchers are endeavouring to understand the origins of the human race, and some are concerned with extra-terrestrial communication with earth, historically and at the present day. However, contact is made mind to mind and only as our minds evolve further will we discover that higher intelligences can shrink time and have made and are making contact with developed humans without the need for space vehicles. My own theory is that many UFOs are holograms to wake people up but not actually physical objects.

In one of our guest bedrooms, I met a German soldier, who was life-size and practically physical, not merely on my inner screen. As a wartime child, I should

---

[87] Maria Callas and I, Sound Healing, Living a Duet for Mankind, Capall Bann Publishing. ISBN 186163274-6
Maria Callas and I on a Sound Healing adventure…A Sequel Capall Bann Publishing 2005 ISBN 1-86163-313-0

have been scared but I wasn't. He said his name was Klaus and asked me to help him clear negative energies by sending light. Our house was built in 1958 on land that had been occupied by German soldiers and building materials had passed close by in railway tracks. There are also dugouts in some nearby gardens and underground tunnels that were closed shortly after the end of the war. In fact, we probably have wartime relics under the ground in our own garden. A friend in a nearby house has a dugout with two underground rooms that she and her husband have turned into a pub with a games and cinema room which is very cheerful and cosy.

During the Occupation, slave labourers building the defences were inhumanly treated and many died from starvation and exhaustion, so it appeared that reparations were being made decades after the end of the war.

However, for the most part, I lived purely in the physical realm. Nevertheless, I am grateful for all I went through in the 1980s and am now aware that reality has many layers and that potentially humans are multidimensional. I have recently cleared the decks and attempt to meditate every day. The regularity is the thing and it certainly helps one's peace of mind, concentration and memory.

Our son, Giles, is now married to Kate and they have twin boys, Charles and Laurence, who were born in March 2014 and they now treat Jersey as their second home.

In 2017, I wrote my first novel, 'Truth Will Find a Way' which has been published by Austin Macauley Publishers Ltd., and the first volume of our joint autobiography, 'Love and Music' was published in April, 2020 by the same publisher. Finally, at long last, the present manuscript entitled Worlds within Worlds, will also be published.

Chapter Twenty-Four
Chapter Coda

Although my husband, Chris, loved coming to Jersey for holidays, he did not find semi-retirement easy. All his professional life he was a singer and a complete man of the theatre. He missed performing, his colleagues and London, though for the first few years here, we went over three to four times a year, staying at the Royal Overseas League, in Mayfair, where we entertained friends and family members and caught up on theatre and art exhibitions. He enjoyed teaching singing but did not have any professional students in Jersey. He broadcast about opera from time to time and enjoyed gardening and crosswords as well as watching cricket on TV. However, his hearing failed in 2010 and his health began to falter with a slight stroke. Nevertheless,, he recovered but gradually became frail, though his brain was as clear as ever and until the last week of his life he was still doing cryptic crosswords.

Finally, his general health failed and he was sent to hospital where he was not expected to live. However, he rallied and was sent home. He regained his voice, which he had lost, and began eating food naturally rather than through a tube and it looked as if he would go on for the foreseeable future but he was living on borrowed time and shortly before Christmas, 2018, he began to fall asleep all the time. Finally, one Monday morning he said he did not want to get up. That was unusual because even when he was really ill, he always wanted to get up, shave and dress. I told him that he should have a lie in, then the doctor and nurse came and I was told that he was seriously ill. His potassium levels were sky high and could not be controlled; this meant that his kidneys and heart were failing. The doctor said we could look after him at home and I was grateful for that. We have a large bedroom with armchairs so we lived upstairs; my office is off the bedroom so I could work at my computer and also keep an eye on Chris. Sometimes I would lie on the bed with him, though he continually slept, and hold his hand and talk to him. It was as if the Angel of Liberation was already in the house because there was a beautiful atmosphere of love and tranquillity and total peace. By Friday, the doctor said he needed a hospital bed so one was brought into our bedroom and Chris was installed in it. The doctor then ordered a Hospice Box to be brought. By Saturday morning, Chris was in more pain than he had ever been, sheer agony, and he called out to me to help him. Finally, I reached the doctor on his mobile phone and he and the nurse came and Chris was given an injection. The doctor told me that he would sleep but his breathing pattern might change, though I was not to be worried by it.

He said I should call our son, Giles, and ask him to come over. He had a concert on that Sunday so could not get away until early Monday morning. I was on my own with Chris for most of the day and I sat and held his hand and talked to him of our happy life together. I told him not to struggle on for me but to fly free.

At about four o'clock our friend, Soula, came and sat with me and we drank tea and talked of her husband and the happy times the four of us had spent together. Don died at home three years ago so Soula had been through what I was experiencing and was very supportive. After a couple of hours, she said: "Listen."

I said I couldn't hear anything. She said that was the point as Chris had stopped breathing. It was all so gentle; he did not even utter a sigh. I had never seen anyone die before and could not believe that it was so easy. Indeed, it made death seem a very little thing. About an hour later, a new doctor came and signed the certificate then the funeral directors arrived. They were very sensitive and carefully took Chris's worn out body to the Chapel of Rest. Soula stayed with me till 11 p.m.

Giles arrived as scheduled early on Monday morning and we planned a service for Chris. It was non-religious; simply recorded music he had loved and two pieces that meant something to him, beautifully read by Giles. Byron's 'So, We'll go no more A-roving' which Chris used to sing so beautifully in Maud Valerie White's lovely setting and Shakespeare's speech, 'Fear no more the heat of the Sun' from 'Cymbeline'. I read a eulogy I had written, outlining Chris's singing career. That was all, no sermon, no hymns, just peace and tranquillity and everyone said that they were moved because there was such an atmosphere of love.

Of all people, I expected him to soon get in touch. When there was no feeling of his presence, I began to wonder what had gone wrong. However, I had not considered that he had died in his sleep. After four months, I awoke early one morning with the tune of the duet 'Love Unspoken' from the 'Merry Widow' on my mind. (This is on YouTube with the Apollo Group Opera Gala from 1998)

We often sang it at concerts and it always brought the house down. Anyway, it meant a lot to us. I sensed that he was using it as a signal. Two days later, as I awoke, I wondered what to wear as I was going out to tea. Then I felt the old 'nudge' and I picked up a notebook and pen; the following is the first 'letter' I received from Chris writing telepathically through me on 7th April 2019 at 07.45 a.m.

I never developed a visual imagination though I loved art and looking at pictures.

However, at first, I was like a newly born kitten whose eyes are not yet open. It was dark, yet I had feelings and suspected there were people around me.

This is why prayers for the dead are valuable; they bring glimpses of light, just small portions at first but gradually one's surroundings become brighter and one is met by those who have come to help you to acclimatise. It takes time and at first, one is inhibited but there is great kindness and understanding. However, one cannot take in too much at once, so one sleeps.

That is a healing process and gradually the new body begins to develop. Yes, it is similar to the old one but without blemish. It feels new, yet at the same time very familiar.

The fact that you concentrate on the Chris you first met means that my body looks very similar now – the old carcass is gone for good and I am quite a handsome chap and much healthier.

Your love and devotion is like food to me and the fact that you constantly think of me so lovingly is the icing on the cake. What a wonderful experience we have had through so many years and not just this time around.

Dear love, I feel I must not tire you – I know you are in constant physical pain (sciatica) but through my love to you, I endeavour to bring you solace.

I am very excited about your writing. You still have a lot to give and more upliftment is coming to you and you will give to others.

You are right, we will challenge Heaven because we cannot let a little thing like death separate us. We are One, a complete entity.

I am only a thought away. I am becoming acclimatised here yet I am ever with you now I have found the way to you and I will write again.

My love to darling Giles, Kate and the boys. Don't let them forget dear old Grandpa. I will watch them with delight. My love to you and all those who remember me. Tell them I am not far away and thank you for all the dear, kind things you say about me – they make me blush yet I love you for it and am so glad that you feel I made life so happy for you.

Well, you did for me, my very dearest darling, and nothing can undo that. Till next time, your ever devoted, loving Chrissie.

24th April 2019 6.30 p.m.

I had been emailing my publisher and starting my income tax return then I took a late lunch on a tray and watched a TV programme. I fell asleep but suddenly I was awoken by almost seeing Chris and someone else come through a window into the room. I thought I must put the kettle on for a cup of tea then I realised that there was no one there.

I was getting over a nasty virus so my defences were low. I had finished the antibiotics the day before. Anyway, I went back to the computer and did some editing of my second volume then rested on the bed for a while. I did not want to read so just lay there thinking of my darling Chris. I began to cry as if my heart would break. Whenever we were apart before I knew, he was still in my world and would return to me, but now, there was a dreadful void. We were always on a mental wavelength but I did not realise how much I would miss his physical presence and our chats when he was gone. Well, suddenly I felt that he was telling me to get my notebook and pen. I picked them up and the following 'letter' came through my hand.

Don't cry, sweetheart, it troubles me to see you so distraught. I too suffer because I miss you so, but truly our hearts are as one and being torn apart physically is the least thing. We are ever entwined in the most important way – our physical selves are purely temporary but our souls are eternal. Be of good cheer – know

I AM NOT FAR, EVEN IF YOU CAN'T SEE ME. I CAN SEE YOU AS IF I HAVE A CRYSTAL BALL, AND I FEEL YOUR LOVE SO STRONGLY; IT IS A POWERFUL SEA THAT ENGULFS ME BUT WITH OVERFLOWING WARMTH.

We cannot truly be parted because as you really know – we are one and the same. Despite loving others our love is paramount and nothing can gainsay it, so my pretty dear; yes, I still think you very pretty because age cannot wither you, your spirit is too strong for that.

Cheer up, Chicken, know that I truly worship you; I adore you as much as ever and even more so because I see right into the heart of you. So, dry your tears, talk to me mentally or aloud and know I am listening.

Don't frown, don't worry, of course, I will be waiting for you when you come over; but you have a little time yet to finish your tasks. I am so proud of you and so grateful for all you did for me throughout our lives together. I am not alone, am not lonely, so don't worry about me. I am in good hands and am now becoming adjusted to my new situation.

More anon; with my most heartfelt love, ever your Chrissie.

I write in longhand and it is like taking dictation. I cannot interrupt the flow which is always very fluid without any corrections or mistakes. It is only when I read it later that it makes sense to me. I type it out so that I can make copies. However, I was taken by surprise to find that a portion was in capitals. That was not me, but evidently, Chris wanted to emphasise the sentence.

Sunday, 28th April 2019, 08.45 a.m

I awoke at 3.15 a.m with the feeling that Chris's energy was filling the room – it was near me, yet expansive. I was aware, yet saw nothing, not even on my inner screen, yet he felt very real.

He was communicating with me but not in the form of a letter, not giving mental dictation. In fact, I felt that he was experiencing difficulty in finding the words to illustrate to me what he wanted to say. He was an educated chap – a Cambridge MA with a well-stocked vocabulary but he did not have words to describe his metaphysical experiences to me, a denizen of the physical world. However, I did get the impression of a vast quantity of light. I did not see it but was aware of it from his point of view. It was Chris alright and he still had his sense of humour but his personality was being absorbed into the light of his Individuality, the permanent part of his eternal essence.

His whole Being, all that he had ever been was being absorbed into the Light. The Individuality is the amalgam of the best qualities of one's past lives and Chris was becoming an expanded soul. In fact, he was being incorporated into his Soul and ultimately into his Spirit – the One Life, made up of all the roles he had played over millennia. This applies to all of us. We are spiritual beings, who, from time to time come to the Earth School to experience and grow through earth lives. It is challenging because we go through so much.

I mentally asked Chris what I should call him now that his personality was absorbed in his Individuality and he made me laugh when he said 'Adonis'. Well, remembering the gorgeous young man I married and how wonderful he looked on the beach, I sometimes refer to him as 'Adonis' and I suppose hearing me say that has amused him. However, I meant it, but now, of course, he is expanding beyond a physical form. However, a few mornings ago, as I awoke I had a clear image on my inner screen of him lying on a rock sunbathing. It was incredibly clear but I could not hold it for more than a few moments, yet it was wonderful.

On Monday this week, my friend Sue B came to give me some Sekem healing for sciatica. She later said that when she came in she expected Chris to make contact. A few weeks ago, we saw the silhouette of a head made of light on the sitting room wall. We could not make out where it came from as it was a dull day. However, she thought it phenomenal and assumed it might be from Chris. She has strong psychic energy herself and as I lay down with my eyes closed and she began the healing, I felt that even though the weather was rather gloomy, the room was full of radiant light and I was in it. Sue felt it too. Suddenly, I realised that I was smiling, then I felt that my aura was blending with that of Chris'. I began to laugh and knew that he was laughing too. It was the most incredible experience because we had become one entity made of abundant light. It was the closest one can ever be to another human being. Now I know that we will always be linked by our eternal love. He tells me that others are coming into my life and they will need my friendship and I have to do my best for them.

I do not feel so much that I have lost him but that his extended self is with me even more, and one day I will join him in my extended self. Life is indeed wonderful.

Though I delayed for years in producing this book, I hope it will bring comfort to those who fear death or have lost loved ones. The most important things are our love links and the fact that our minds determine how and where we find ourselves after we leave this level. It seems that even our beloved pets can follow us into the beyond if we love them enough.

My experiences have taken me further away from orthodox religion because for me it doesn't go far enough. So much is missing, particularly regarding re-incarnation which explains much that is otherwise inexplicable. My whole life has been a search for truth and still, it goes on.

There is a huge amount of illness in the world today; as well as conflict, while at the same time, there is a growing hunger for spirituality. During my long life, I have learned many things that are not on the syllabus of any university. I am eternally grateful to my unseen teachers and friends who have taught me that death is not the end, merely another beginning. I am also aware that although our bodies sleep during the night, our consciousness continues learning and communes with those more spiritually evolved than we are.

The deep, inexplicable yearnings we sometimes feel are divine discontent, the longing of the soul for its eternal home. We are spiritual beings experiencing a physical world but it is not our real home, and when we lose touch with our inner self, depression and ill health result.

Everyone is on a spiritual journey, even those who are totally unaware of the fact. Our experiences are unique to each of us because we are all individuals, yet the goal is the same – to be re-united with the Source of all Being. However, there is no rush because we have all of eternity to experience the journey.

Once in a meditation session, I felt as if my heart had burst asunder and I was in a state of consciousness that was beyond duality. It was like Mother Julian had stated: "All is well and all will be well". I had no idea where I was unless it was the Nirvana, sages speak of.

I only know that there were no worries, no conflicts, no dark or light, only perfect unity, which brought to mind the phrase 'the Peace that Passeth Understanding'.

Since 1982, when Maria manifested through Christine, my far memory has opened up and I am aware of several past incarnations. I realise that I, like everyone else, have played and will play many parts. The spiritual individuality (which has its own name) equals the actor who dons a costume and plays the role of a particular character for a certain time, then when the play is done, takes off his costume and returns home. Later, he accepts another role in another costume; thus the experiences of the actor are absorbed into the eternal individuality.

The initiate who penned the Shakespeare plays was aware of this aspect when he declared, "All the world's a stage and the men and women, merely players."

There is a design behind the sequence of lives we take on to promote balance. A serving maid in one life may become the mistress in the next one. No one is tied down to a particular section of society forever because we need to experience all aspects of life on earth.

My inner memories have been gently awoken and gradually more information is revealed. At first, it was quite confusing but little by little, it began to make sense because I saw from where I derived my talents, interests, likes, dislikes, and the places, as well as people, that resonate with me in my present life. When I attended a weekend workshop on exploring past lives at the College of Psychic Studies, I already knew something about my immediate past life as a female singer and an earlier one as a man. In the sessions with Harry, the workshop leader, there was no hypnotism involved, merely a deeply relaxed meditative state. Forty of us were involved and Harry used the material which came to light as part of a serious scientific research programme. The quality of the information that came through was undeniable and in some cases, verifiable.

In my own case, what surprised me was the third life which came to light near the end of the last session. It transpired that my 'life of achievement' was that of a nun in a small convent at St. Pere, (I even said it was two kilometres from Vezelay). At the time, I had no idea where Vezelay was but I was euphoric when I returned to the present, so full of joy that I felt I could fly. To all intents and purposes, it was a simple life, in a small convent which I entered at about the age of fourteen. I had been taught Latin as a child and though I first worked in the infirmary, tending the old and sick, I began to grow herbs in a knot garden.

Past life resonances continued to come to the surface and I have been back to St. Pere in Burgundy several times, not only with Jill but with Chris and Jane, and have seen the little churchyard where the nuns are buried. However, the wrought iron gate is always locked and the graves are overgrown so I have not been able to ascertain if my little nun is buried there. Mind you, I am not sure of her name, but it sounds something like Dorillia. That life, simple as it was, has given me many 'Brownie points', which I am still reaping.

Looking back, I now realise that my own spiritual awakening began when I started to pray for wisdom. The Bible says, 'Ask and you will receive' and it is said that when the student is ready, the teacher appears. I now know that both sayings are true.

Despite my 'otherworldly' experiences, I have never lost sight of my inner child and I enjoy playing with the dolls' houses in my large collection. Since the age of six, when I was given my first dolls' house, I have been an enthusiast and three days after moving to Jersey I joined the Jersey Dolls' House and Miniatures Club, with whom I enjoy monthly meetings and preparing for our bi-annual exhibitions where we raise money for various charities.

Unfortunately, at the moment we are in lock-down due to the Corona Virus, so everything is in abeyance, but it is hoped that at last our activities can resume.

Life continues to be fascinating and I am blessed with wonderful friends, here in Jersey, the UK and further afield, who have been wonderfully supportive to me in my recent widowhood. I trust that I will also be a firm support to those in similar circumstances. It is true what the Native Americans say: "To truly understand another person you have to walk in their moccasins for at least two weeks."

My dear husband, was the most understanding of men. He never judged anyone, and he never criticised or tried to change me. He told a friend that he appreciated the fact that I always gave him space, but then he did the same for me.

He taught me so much and I never cease to be grateful for his devoted love, which I am sure accompanies me now and always.